IMPOSTERS
in the
OVAL OFFICE

IMPOSTERS
in the
OVAL OFFICE

ROBERT C. LAITY

IMPOSTERS IN THE OVAL OFFICE

iUniverse books may be ordered through booksellers or by contacting:

iUniverse
1663 Liberty Drive
Bloomington, IN 47403
www.iuniverse.com
1-800-Authors (1-800-288-4677)

ISBN: 978-1-5320-5436-5 (sc)
ISBN: 978-1-5320-5435-8 (e)

Library of Congress Control Number: 2018909780

Print information available on the last page.

iUniverse rev. date: 08/15/2018

Pursuant to Article II, Sec. 1, clause 5 and the 12th Amendment of the United States Constitution, **only** a Natural Born U.S. Citizen can be President. Being a "natural born citizen" is the highest level of citizenship which exists. The legally established definition of what a Natural Born Citizen is will be discussed in this book. This eligibility requirement applies to only two positions in the entire federal government., that of President and Vice-President of the United States of America.

Why would the Founders insist that the Presidency devolve only upon a person who is a one hundred percent American?

It's so that there would be no possibility of any foreign influence being interjected into the workings of our sovereign government. It was John Jay who first very strongly suggested that our President should be a "Natural Born Citizen".

Originally the text of the constitution required the same level of citizenship that a Senator or Representative had to possess. That of "Citizen". That would have meant that a President need not have even been born here. Many "Citizens" are not born in the United States and have attained that citizenship by naturalization.

John Jay did not believe that it was appropriate to allow a naturalized Citizen to be President. He wanted a higher standard of citizenship involved. What circumstances would have to be met in order to assure that there would be no doubt that our President had only American ties and loyalties?

Jay came up with requiring a President and Vice-President to be a "Natural Born Citizen". A Natural Born American would be a 100% American. He/she would be "Of the Blood" of Americans and "Of the soil" of America. He/she would have both Jus Soli and 100% Jus Sanquinis. No other type of Citizenship would suffice.

John Jay, one of the founders was also our nation's first Chief Justice of the United States of America. The other signers of the U.S. Constitution agreed with John Jay and they incorporated the mandatory criteria that a President must be born in the United States to Parents who were both American citizens themselves. Indeed, this is what all the founders knew as the definition of what a natural born citizen is.

In the 18th Century, French was the language of Diplomacy. Many of the founders spoke French, especially Benjamin Franklin who served as an ambassador to France. There was a book, written in French and later translated into English, that Mr. Franklin brought back with him from Europe and that is still being used to this day. It is the same book that George Washington, our first U.S. President borrowed from the New York Society Library on October 5, 1789 and did not return. In the recent past, that Library was given another copy of the same edition of the book "Law of Nations". The overdue fees of $300,000 were not requested by the Library but I would reasonably conjecture that a 1789 edition of the treatise would be worth as much or more. In French the "Law of Nations" is called "Les droits de Gens ou principe de le loi naturelle". The Law of Nations is also incorporated into our constitution by reference at Article 1, Clause 8. It was translated from Latin into French by Emerlich Vattel. It was not originally written by him and has roots in Roman Law.

In the 18th century the book was ubiquitously used by both U.S. and British courts. It was then widely known and understood that a natural born citizen is one born in a country to parents who were both citizens of said country. In the original French the definition of a "Natural Born Citizen" is written "Les naturelles, ou indigenes, sont ceux qui sont, nes dans le pays de Parents Citoyens". The English translation is "The Natural born are those born in a country to parents who are both citizens".

Several United States Supreme Court opinions have affirmed and reaffirmed this definition of what a "Natural Born Citizen" is. In one case, ***Minor v Happersett, 88US, 162***,(1875) the U.S.

Supreme Court unanimously opined that a "Natural Born Citizen" is "One born in the United States to Parents who are [both] U.S. Citizens themselves". This opinion was reaffirmed in subsequent U.S. Supreme Court decisions in the Venus, Shanks v Dupont and Wong Kim Ark. The prior cases were left undisturbed in Laity v NY, 13-875, USSCt.,cert.denied (2014).

It follows that anyone who was not born in the United States to Parents who were both U.S. Citizens themselves is not eligible to be President of the United States or for that matter, Vice-President of the United States.

In 1787 there were no "Natural Born" Citizens in the United States that met all the Article II, Sec. 1 Clause 5 criteria to be President or Vice-President. The founders understood this. They acted to grandfather in those persons who have stood for the cause of the American Revolution and Independence from England. Our first "Natural Born" Citizen President, who met all of the Article II criteria, was Martin Van Buren, born in 1782 in the United States to Parents who were both U.S.

Citizens themselves. Every other President since Van Buren, has been born in the United States to Parents who were both U.S. Citizens themselves **except** two persons, who attained to the Presidency & who did **not meet** the Constitutional criteria. Barack Obama and Chester Arthur managed fraudulently to attain to the office of the Presidency and to usurp the office. They both were therefore, not bona-fide Presidents.

The usurpation of our highest office did not happen just once in our history, with Chester A. Arthur in 1881. It was allowed by nonfeasant powers that be to happen again with Barack H. Obama, one hundred and twenty seven years later in 2008 and once again in 2012. The first usurper Chester A. Arthur was born in the United States on October 5th,1829. His Father William Arthur, was born in Dreen, Ireland and was a British Subject. The fact that William Arthur did not naturalize as a U.S. Citizen until a full (14) years after Chester's birth in Vermont, disqualified Chester A. Arthur from being President of the United States. Chester was (14) years old already when William finally naturalized as a U.S. Citizen. Both Chester Arthur and Barack Obama unconstitutionally, illegally and illicitly exercised the authority of the Presidency. Authority that legally they did not have nor were ever entitled to.

Neither of the two was ever the bona-fide President of the United States.

Chester Arthur, "President #21" and Barack Obama "President #43" were counterfeit Presidents. They were never legally elected because they did not meet constitutional muster. That they do not meet the criteria set forth by law means that they were not bona-fide Presidents. Not being a Natural Born Citizen is a deficiency in meeting constitutional criteria, the same as if a President weren't thirty five years old or fourteen years a resident of the U.S. Obama and Arthur failed to meet all (3) mandatory criteria in Article II, Sec. 1, Clause 5 to qualify as eligible to be President.

Chester Arthur destroyed the proof that would warrant his vacating of the Office of the Presidency. Regardless, It was discovered after his death when it surfaced that he was not a "Natural Born" Citizen of the U.S. It was too late to do anything to stop Chester Arthur. However, it was not and is not too late to bring Barack H. Obama to justice. Obama is not a "Natural Born" U.S. Citizen. He said so himself on several occasions alluding to his "Kenyan and Indonesian roots".

Obama claims that his Father was Barack Obama, Sr. and his Mother was Stanley Dunham. There is no acceptable or confirmable proof that these persons were Barack Obama, Jr's actual parents. The Birth Certificate that Obama, Jr. proffered has been found by several independent and competent forensic document experts to be a forgery. This has been confirmed by separate forensic studies.

A very extensive investigation of Obama was undertaken by then Sheriff of Maricopa County, Arizona, Joseph Arpaio and his Cold Case Posse. The fact that Obama's birth certificate and other documents that he proffered such as his selective service card, are forgeries belies Obama's claim that he is a natural born citizen of the U.S.

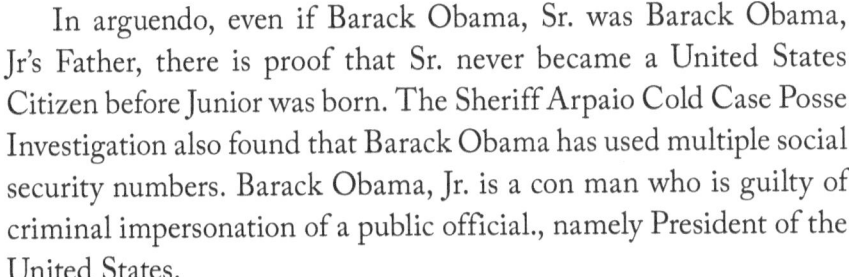

In arguendo, even if Barack Obama, Sr. was Barack Obama, Jr's Father, there is proof that Sr. never became a United States Citizen before Junior was born. The Sheriff Arpaio Cold Case Posse Investigation also found that Barack Obama has used multiple social security numbers. Barack Obama, Jr. is a con man who is guilty of criminal impersonation of a public official., namely President of the United States.

The fact that he usurped the Presidency during wartime compounds the crime and makes it espionage and treason.

It is a violation of the DC Code and at a higher level, espionage and treason, which are felonies under 18USC, Part 1, Chapter 115, Sec.2381 and 10USC, Section 906, Article 106, Spies.

Barack Obama usurped the Presidency during time of war.

Let's review what 10USC says about "Any person" being in any place, wherein the conduct of war is engaged in, without legal authorization and elaborate on what sort of place the law is referring to,10USC, Section 906, Article 106. Spies., reads:

> *"ANY person who in time of war is found lurking as a spy or acting as a spy in or about any place, vessel, or aircraft within the control or jurisdiction of the armed forces, or in and about any shipyard, any manufacturing or industrial plant, or any other place or institution engaged in work in aid of the prosecution of the war, by the United States, or elsewhere shall be tried by a General Court-Martial or by a military commission and on conviction shall be punished by death…"*

The particular wording of the Statute, otherwise known as the Uniform Code of Military Justice, in Section 906 refers to "**Any Person…**". This means that **it applies to both military personnel and non-military personnel (civilians).**

"**Who in time of war**" means when the United States and/or it's Military is engaged in combat or war with a foreign armed force such as we have been in Iraq and Afghanistan for (15) yrs.

"**Is found lurking as a spy or acting as a spy**" means a person who, without legal authority, lurks [or enters] in a restricted area and/or presents a threat to National Security.

"**Any place...within the control or jurisdiction of the Armed forces...**" means in such places as the Pentagon, aboard or near a Naval vessel, the White House War room, briefings, and the like.

All should agree that a person who was not elected legally because he/she does not meet Constitutional muster under Article II, Sec. 1, Clause 5 is **not legally authorized** to be in restricted areas and has absolutely no level of clearance to review our nations classified information. He/she is therefore, if during time of war, a spy.

I consulted with a Marine Judge Advocate General Officer. I am on solid ground here. Barack Obama is a spy. Is Barack Obama also a traitor under 18USC, Part 1, Chapter 115, Sec. 2381? I say that he is one. I am not the sole individual to accuse Barack Obama of Treason. Charges against Obama were formally lodged by several persons in the past and the charges have been on record for at least (9) years now. Let us review what the Treason statute reads:

> "**Whoever, owing allegiance to the** United **States,** levies war against them or adheres to their enemies, giving them aid and comfort within the United States or elsewhere, is guilty of treason and shall suffer death, or shall be imprisoned for not less than five years and fined under this title but not less than $10,000; and shall be **incapable of holding any office under the United States**"

Barack Obama, by virtue of having taken the oath of Office, owes allegiance to the United States. He violated the oath of Office knowing that he was not eligible to be President of theUnited States because he is not an Article II, "Natural Born Citizen" of the United States. Obama by his usurpation of the Presidency, during time of war, became a spy the moment he entered into the Office of the

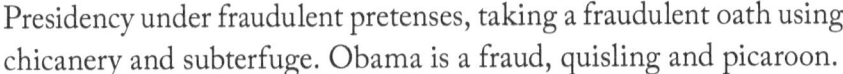

Presidency under fraudulent pretenses, taking a fraudulent oath using chicanery and subterfuge. Obama is a fraud, quisling and picaroon.

His deliberate criminal actions, and other crimes are felonious and amount to giving aid and comfort to America's enemies during time of war. His treasonous acts immediately proscribed any entitlement that he may have ever had to hold **"Any office under the United States"**. Obama was never for one second eligible to be President of the United States.

Obama does not meet Article II criteria of being a "Natural Born Citizen". Pure and simple he's as phony as a $3 bill.

So, what again is a **"Natural Born" Citizen?** It has been established by the U.S. Supreme Court that a "Natural Born" Citizen is one born IN the United States **in addition to** having been born of parents who were both U.S. Citizen's themselves at time of birth of said person.

The Constitution states that Congressmen and Senators must only be "Citizens" of the United States. However, it requires that Presidents and Vice-Presidents be "Natural Born" citizens. So, what is a "Citizen" as opposed to a "Natural Born Citizen"? A "Citizen" is one that meets any of a number of statutory naturalization requirements that can be met in a number of ways to become a U.S. Citizen.

A naturalized "Citizen" is not tantamount to a "Natural Born" Citizen, however, nor is one who is solely "Born a citizen" who has only U.S. jus soli, being "of the soil" of the U.S. A Natural Born Citizen must meet the other criteria for being a "Natural Born Citizen". Namely one must be a 100% American, having jus sanquinis, which is "of the blood" of Americans along with U.S. jus soli, which is "of the soil".

One can become a Statutory Citizen by solely being born here, jus soli or by having one U.S. Citizen Parent under certain conditions, 50% jus sanquinis or by other means of naturalization. However, these persons are not 100% Americans. They are not "Natural Born" citizens unless they are born in the United States, in addition to being born to parents who were both U.S. Citizens themselves at the time of birth of the person. There is nothing difficult about understanding the differences between the terms "Born a Citizen", "Citizen" and "Natural Born Citizen".

All Natural Born Citizens are Citizens but all Citizens are not Natural Born Citizens. There is absolutely nothing that anyone can do., no steps that can be taken, to make a "Natural Born Citizen" out of someone who was not born in the United States to Parents who were both U.S. Citizens themselves. Only those born under those very specific circumstances are Natural Born Citizens., no one else.

Who is Barack H.Obama, Jr. really?

Very few people really know who Barack Obama, Jr. really is. I wonder if he even knows who he is with all the plethora of mendacities that he has proffered over the last decade or more. His Birth certificate has been deemed a forgery by competent and independent forensic document examiners. If the forged birth certificate is all Obama has then he has no real proof that he is the son of Barack Obama, Sr. and Stanley Dunham. His Birth Certificate is a forgery. The information on it cannot be verified or trusted.

A broad effort must be undertaken to determine just who Obama really is. There is information in the public domain showing that Stanley Dunham was associated with an Indonesian cult called Subud. Stanley Dunham was a loose woman. Pictures of her posing nude are in the public domain and available on the internet. It would be an easy task to have recruited her to play the part and claim that she was Obama's Mother or alternatively falsely confirm Barack Obama, Sr. as Junior's father. It has been conjectured that Barack may be the son of Mohammad Sumohadiwidjojo the Subud cult leader.

Indeed, Ms. Loretta Fuddy, the deceased former Director of Hawaiian Vital Statistics, who purportedly "accidently" drowned in a plane crash was also associated with Subud along with Stanley Dunham. Subud had people in Indonesia, Hawaii and Seattle, Washington, all places that Stanley Dunham had community ties to.

There are so many unanswered questions about Barack Obama, Jr. aka Barry Soetoro, aka Barack "X" Shabazz, aka Barrack Sumohadiwidjojo aka Barack Davis. Who knows who Obama really is? Barack Obama even resembles Osama Bin Laden. I would like to see forensic proof that Osama Bin Laden is dead or that he died in the manner claimed by Obama. Obama has dressed in Muslim Garb before and it wouldn't be the first time some master spy/disguise artist pulled the wool over America's eyes. It seems that many people do not really care who Obama really is. I care and so should you.

The requirement that a President be 100% American is a great one. We had a Muslim spy named Obama in the Oval Office for (8) years undermining the United States every chance that he got. Article II of the Constitution was written, for a very good reason. Requiring that a President be a "Natural Born Citizen" was/is necessary to the integrity of our Presidency. It has been usurped twice since 1889. Let me say that again and please let that sink in. **"Our Presidency has been usurped twice"** by people with foreign ties.

Attempts were made in the 2016 elections to do it again. Many of our American ancestors shed their blood and lost their lives defending and preserving our American republic for posterity. The word posterity means America's children. Our parents passed the torch of freedom and liberty to us. They spent their lives preserving the Nation's freedoms. Now, it's our responsibility to maintain, preserve and protect it so that it will continue to flourish for another 240 years and more. Our republic must be kept. It cannot be ignored. Freedom is fragile. If we lose the republic it will not be easily recovered.

You would not hand the keys to your home to a stranger. Why would you allow unknown interlopers to overthrow our nation with impunity under color of law? That's just bizarre and insane. It's national suicide, the facilitation of the demise of the United States of America. Obama is an infiltrator. Both major parties stacked the deck in favor of the shadow Government, in the 2008 and 2012 presidential election. The two major parties **both** proffered constitutionally barred candidates. Again, both John McCain and Barack Obama are ineligible to be President. Neither of them are "Natural Born Citizens". Obama's purported father was never naturalized and McCain was born in Colon, Panama. McCain lacks U.S. jus soli and if one were to concede that Stanley and Barry, Sr were Junior's parents, then Obama lacks 100% jus sanquinis and U.S.

jus soli. I won't go into it in detail here but there is an official claim that Hawaii, purported place of Obama's birth, **may not even be a State, that it was illegally annexed by the United States.** See: "The Apology", PL103-150 signed by William Clinton as President on November 23, 1993

I Have been working on this case for over (9) years now. I started on or about November 2, 2008. I knew that Obama was a phony from the outset of his campaign. Many other people knew it too. Scores if not hundreds of cases have been filed in the courts since 2008. There are several cases still proceeding in the courts. One of those is Laity v. New York State, Rafael "Ted" Cruz, Marco Rubio and Piyash "Bobby" Jindal now at the NY State Court of Appeals.

Rafael "Ted" Cruz was born in Canada. That disqualifies him for the Presidency on that fact alone. His father was a Cuban-Canadian at the time of "Ted" Cruz's birth in Canada. Cruz's Mother was an American but later went to Canada, Ted Cruz always tries to impress people that he is a so called "Constitutional Scholar". Funny, Obama claims the same thing. Cruz wants to be President but can't even adhere to one little old Article of it if that non-adherence serves himself.

Former U.S. Senator Bob Dole said that "Cruz entered the U.S. Senate as a Canadian". Cruz wasn't even a bona-fide U.S. Senator.

Piyash "Bobby" Jindal is out as a President. Both of his parents were citizen's of India when he was born.

Marco Rubio's is ineligible to be President because both his parents were Cuban citizen's when Marco was born. Marco Rubio's parents were not U.S. Citizens. They were permanent residents. Permanent residents in the U.S. are not Citizens of the United States.

Another ineligible person who has recently looked into becoming President was Arnold Swarzenegger

It can be easily confirmed that Congress has attempted at least (8) or more time since the late 1970s to do away with the Natural Born Citizen requirement to be President. All attempts have failed.

Only persons intent on eroding our firewalls want to weaken such a strong check and balance against usurpation of our Presidency.

It is apparent that since the "deep state" has been unsuccessful in doing so, in the legislative process, that they are now overtly flouting the Constitution.

Since October, 2017 the Court of Appeals of the State of New York has been deliberating for the purpose of determining whether there is a constitutional issue on the subject of New York State's Board of Election's outright, overt and deliberate misrepresentation of the criteria for being President. As I said, the U.S. Constitution mandates that a President and anyone who attains to that Office must be a "Natural Born Citizen".

New York State has been misstating the legal requirement as being "born a Citizen" for almost a decade or more.

As explained earlier, one who is "born a Citizen" is not necessarily a "Natural Born Citizen". It should be restated that the United States Constitution requires a candidate for President and/or Vice President to be a "Natural Born Citizen".

I have also moved the court to find Respondents Rafael "Ted" Cruz, Marco Rubio and Piyash "Bobby" Jindal guilty of attempting to repeat what Arthur and Obama did., usurp the Presidency by fraud.

Their actions demonstrated that the checks and balances that our founders incorporated in the cherished document known as the Constitution of the United States of America have since eroded. No one in authority in the 2008 and 2012 election thought to ensure that the Constitutional protections afforded by the "Natural Born Citizen" clause were being adhered to.

No one, of course, but me and a very conscientious and patriotic band of Americans who have been actively seeking that this issue of grave national security import be finally addressed in the serious manner it deserves.

Had one of the three recent usurperous candidates succeeded to become a **third** imposter in our presidency, that would have been our third strike. As we all know, "Three Strikes and you're out" works both in baseball and in the law. When (3) fraudulent bunco artists succeed in taking over the reins of the most powerful nation on Earth, without any adverse repercussions, that is simply unconscionable and cannot be tolerated. It must be addressed by Lady Justice.

We the People must not allow this demonstrable pattern of abrogating Article II, Sec. 1, Clause 5 to continue unabated and any public official, whose duty it is to order it to cease and desist, who does not do so immediately is complicit, guilty of misprision of felony, espionage and treason.

Those officials would be nonfeasant in office as well. Judges, Military Personnel, Executive Branch Officials, Legislators and Law Enforcement Officials all take Oaths of office that they are legally and morally bound and required to adhere to and to honor. Public officials who do not adhere to the U.S. Constitution are derelict in their duty to uphold it. I take my duty to do so very seriously.

When I first started blowing the whistle on Obama, I was on Topix and Twitter writing things like Obama belongs in jail and that he is a fraud, traitor and a spy. I said what I am still saying. Obama stands accused of Treason, Espionage and usurpation of the Presidency during wartime. He is a person of interest in several execution style murders and other heinous crimes. I said that if convicted, Obama should hang by the neck until dead or be shot to death by a military firing squad.

That got me a visit from two Secret Service Agents. Agents from the Buffalo, New York Secret Service field office. One of those agents was Greg Gramiccioni. They came knocking on my door one morning. One of my Brothers in Law was at the house at the time. The door was a bit ajar and I was on my La-Z-Boy recliner relaxing when they came. I called out and told them to come in. It was a bit chilly so I had my arms inside my shirt to keep warm. Agent G. told me that I "best be taking your arms out of that shirt". I had already been in the process of doing so. Agent G. seemed a bit antsy.

The agents started asking me questions which I answered freely. I told them that I had no intention of harming Obama nor did my comments on twitter and topix rise to that level. The fact is that the death penalty is on the table should Obama be convicted of being a traitor and a spy and for usurping the Presidency during war time. I merely stated that.

During the visit by the Secret Service, my brother in law had gone to the Bathroom. As he was coming out of the Loo, Agent G asked "who is that?" I noticed Agent G getting antsy again with his hand by his gun.

I said relax, that's my brother in law Bill. He's visiting. The agents looked around my house and asked a few more questions. We engaged in a little small talk. I told him about how I believe that Obama was an imposter in the White House and that the secret service was putting their lives on the line for an imposter in the oval office. Agent G responded that "That's above [his] pay grade".

They were talking with my brother in law for a few moments and told him that "should I leave town" that they "want to know about it". They wanted him to report to them.

Strangely, after a little bit of time had passed after that visit, my car was stopped by the police. I wasn't driving the car. I had lent it to my sister and her husband. They were questioned about me and about my car. My sister and her husband were told to go on their way after it was found that I was not driving it. I surmise the Secret Service was keeping tabs on me and that they were nervous because it was around the same time that Obama, had come to Western New York by motorcade and had just left the area.

Getting back to the particular secret service visit, the time came when the agents left. I said call me before you come next time. I will make coffee. I know from my (40) years experience working in the federal sector in the U.S. Navy, the U.S. Postal service and the Department of Veterans Affairs that feds like coffee and drink a lot of it.

I had later called Agent Gramiccioni with some follow-up information. He called back and left a message on my answer machine that he wanted "to talk to me". I believe he thought that I would be too intimidated to call him back.But, I did call him back. He never responded.

When I had wanted too file a complaint against Obama with the FBI, they once told me that they "don't take complaints. We just investigate". What do they investigate if they don't take complaints?

Prior to the visit from the Secret Service agents I had been visited one morning by two DOJ agents. I let them in to my home and we talked. They asked me questions about my emotional health, if I owned any guns., the usual questions federal agents ask. I told them of my concerns. One of the agents told me that I was "not the only one with such concerns". Apparently satisfied that I had no intent on doing any harm to Obama and that I was totally relying of the long arm of the law to catch up to Obama, the agents left my home. They asked if they could come back in the future and I said yes.

I told them what I would later tell the two Secret Service agents., for them to call me first the next time they visit so that I could make coffee. The DOJ agents then walked away.

The reason that the DOJ agents visited me to begin with, was to follow up on a formal Tonawanda Police complaint against Obama that I filed circa 2010. That complaint, at my request, was forwarded through the Chief of Tonawanda Police to Chief Lanier of the D.C. Police. It also was assigned a temporary log in number of T14002751.

That filing was made on the advice of Magistrate Judges Leslie Foschio and Kenneth Schroeder of the U.S.District Court for the Western District of New York, whom I first appeared before seeking to swear out an AO91- federal criminal information against bogus Barry Obama. I had approached all the local magistrates and Justices in the U.S.District Court-WDNY. Every last one of them. Judges Schroeder and Foschio put me on the right course to pursue my charges against Obama. They told me that I couldn't swear out a complaint before them., it was up to the U.S. Attorney, at the time, Ms. Mehltretter. She was provided a copy of a notarized sworn AO91 (Federal Criminal Information) against Obama, sworn out by me, which the U.S.D.C. Judges and Magistrates said they could not accept.

Judge Schroeder told me that my first step would be to file a complaint with "local law enforcement" which I did. I filed a formal police report against Obama with the City of Tonawanda New York Police Department Chief. The Chief of Police forwarded my charges to the FBI and Secret Service. On my request the charges were sent to Chief Lanier of the D.C. Police from the Chief of Police in Tonawanda, NY.

Nine years later I am still trying to get the message across to the nation that the founders placed into the U.S. Constitution, "checks and balances", for a reason. These are such things as the Congress holding the purse strings and the judicial branch considering the constitutionality of the Laws that Congress writes as well as the President having veto power and power to issue executive orders.

These measures were put in the U.S. Constitution in order so that concentration of power would not settle in one person or in one branch over another. A very important check was one that proscribes anyone from becoming the President and Commander in Chief of the U.S. Armed services unless he/she is born in the United States to Parents who were both U.S. Citizens themselves. The reader must agree that if any ineligible foreigner were allowed to attain to the Presidency it would be as if we opened up our doors to foreign invasion.

The founders would never have allowed any British Citizen/ Subject to become our President. Yet there have been two persons in our Presidency who were born after 1787 with dual U.S./ British Subject /citizenship and who were not "Natural Born [U.S.] Citizens". They were Chester Arthur "President #21" and Barack Hussein Obama "President#43". Neither Arthur or Obama were ever the legally bona-fide President of the United States of America.

Research has shown that every President, from Martin Van Buren, President #8, except for Chester Arthur and Barack Obama and the first (7) Presidents who were grandfathered in, had Parents who were both U.S. Citizens themselves. They were all born in the United States to parents who were themselves, U.S. Citizens.

Barack Obama's birth circumstances are in serious doubt since the findings of the Sheriff Arpaio Cold Case Posse determined that Barack Obama, Jr's Birth Certificate is a shoddy forgery as is his

Selective Service card and the fact that Obama has used another person's Social Security number. Obama's purported father Barack Obama, Sr. was never a U.S. Citizen.

Chester A. Arthur's father,William, was born in Dreen, Ireland and was not a citizen of the U.S. until a full (14) years after Chester was born. Neither Arthur or Obama were alive at the signing of the Declaration of Independence. Only the founders were grandfathered in by the Constitution and did not have to be "Natural Born Citizens" to be President. The first (7) U.S. Presidents were not NBCs.

The constitution strengthens the Presidency by mandating that Presidents and Vice-Presidents are legally required to be "Natural Born" Citizens. (See the 12th Amendment). A "Natural Born" Citizen is "One born in the United States to parents who are both U.S. Citizens themselves. See: Minor v Happersett, U.S. Supreme Court.

Those of us who care about defending the Constitution and upholding it, sought avenues that we could take in order to bring Barack Obama, Jr. to the Bar of Justice. No one is above the law.

One of those avenues was a Non-Judicial Citizen Empaneled Grand Jury "Presentment" hearing to investigate whether enough evidence exists to "Present" it to a Federal Grand Jury.

What is a "Citizen's empaneled grand jury Presentment hearing", you might ask? I will tell you.

In 1946 the Federal Rules of Criminal Procedure were promulgated. Errant rule makers of the FRCrimP erroneously and unconstitutionally did away with panels called Grand Jury Presentment Hearings which were, as a matter of course, processed with no Judicial intervention, interference or input.

These panels were strictly made up of citizens only. No attorneys, prosecutors or judges were involved or even permitted to be in a Presentment hearing. Prior to 1946 these citizen panels were in ubiquitous usage all over the United States and were bona-fide pursuant to the constitutional authority vested in "We the People" by the fifth amendment, to remove malfeasant Judges and derelict public officials. Corrupt public officials and Judges were actually removed from office using this power. There came a time when those corrupt officials,in 1946, fearing the power of "We the People", a power which we still have under 5A, to check any abusive wielding of authority by the powers that be, acted to call the hearings "Obsolete" and illegally stifled them.

The authority for citizen empaneled Presentment hearings still exists under the fifth Amendment. They needed only to be taken off the shelf, dusted off and used again. With that in mind several American Grand Jury Panels were instituted in 2008 to hear the evidence against Barack Obama. They were properly empaneled by the power vested in the People by the fifth Amendment. I served on two of these panels.

All the jury members of these several panels took oaths of jurists and our charge was to consider all the evidence against Barack Obama, who at the time had been accused of Treason, fraud, usurpation of the Presidency and other crimes. The Presentments that resulted from the hearings which found against Barack Obama were then given to law enforcement, public officials, news media and elected officials.

These hearings took place in the late 2K aughts. An FBI complaint with thousands of signatories was given to then FBI director Mueller. I am signatory number 1501 of 3150.

Usurpation of the Presidency during war time is espionage. That carries the death penalty under 10USC, Sec. 906, Article 106, Spies. Deliberately betraying the United States and giving aid and comfort to the enemy is Treason under 18USC, Part 1, Chapter 115, Sec. 2381. Obama is a domestic enemy.

Again, I was on two Citizen's Grand Juries. I saw quite a bit of evidence against Barack Obama. Barack Obama is a fraud, usurper, traitor and spy. He is guilty of espionage and treason against the United States.

There were many complaints filed with the FBI, the Secret Service, the DC Police, the Tonawanda, NY Police, several Public officials, the US attorney for DC, and the AG of the United States. There were scores of lawsuits by several prominent attorneys and pro se litigants. I personally have sued Obama several times.

Nothing much, if anything, has been done by the powers that be to prosecute Obama. Obama was placed under formal citizen's arrest, by me, in 2012. Service of legal notice to that effect was made on Eric Holder, the AG of the U.S.

Obama belongs in the brig at Ft. Leavenworth or Guantanamo Bay. What Obama did, usurp the Presidency during war time, is a capital offense. Those of us who have sought to do our civic duty as Americans have been met with a wall of obstruction-ism and we have been labeled as "Birthers".

The law is the law. Obama and Arthur were not eligible to be President of the United States. Founding Father David Ramsay who wrote "A dissertation on the manner of acquiring the character and privileges of a citizen of the United States" (1789), said that: "The [U.S.] citizenship of no man could be previous to the Declaration of Independence, and as a **natural right,** belongs to none then those who have been born of citizens [in the U.S.] since the Fourth of July,1776".

In the Naturalization Act of 1790 Congress wrote a provision of the act that only **"considered"** persons who were born "beyond the seas" to two American Parents, as being "Natural Born Citizens". Those who use this in an argument in defense of John McCain always neglect to inform anyone that just a mere (5) years passed before, in the Nationality Act of 1795, that very provision was **repealed as an unconstitutional mistake, an error.**

Natural Born Citizens are only those who are born in the United States to Parents who are both U.S. Citizen's themselves. Pursuant to these facts, John McCain cannot be President or Vice-President either.

Now, one might ask, why is John McCain ineligible to be President of the United States? I will tell you why.

Although John McCain's Parents were both U.S. Citizens, John McCain was not born in the United States of America or in one of it's incorporated Territories.

At the time of the writing of this book the United States had only one incorporated territory That is Palmyra atoll. The U.S, at the time of this writing, has five unincorporated territories.

They are Puerto Rico, U.S. Virgin Islands, Guam, The Northern Mariana Islands and American Samoa. For purposes of satisfying the Article II, Sec. 1 "Natural Born Citizen" requirement to be President, birth in an unincorporated territory does not qualify as birth in the United States of America.That should answer Congressman Serrano's question.

Unincorporated territories are not part of the United States as a whole. They are not "incorporated". People born in an unincorporated territory of the U.S. are not born in the United States but are statutory citizens (Naturalized).

Noteworthy is that a person born on the Palmyra Atoll would be born in the United States since Palmyra Atoll is a fully incorporated territory of the U.S. If said person were born on Palmyra Atoll to Parents who were both U.S. Citizens then said person would be a "Natural Born Citizen" just as if he/she were born in any State.

John McCain was born outside the Panama Canal Zone in Colon, Panama. Panama was never a territory of the United States and Colon, Panama as well as Panama City, Panama, were never a part of the Panama Canal Zone. Those two major Panamanian cities were excluded from the parameters of the PCZ by treaty. That makes John McCain ineligible to be President or Vice-President. Did he know that he too is ineligible when he ran against Barack Obama? The fact is that both major parties proffered constitutionally barred candidates to be President in 2008. That fact makes the 2008 Election a bi-partisan scam and farce.

There was a comment by one Judi Murthi, in the Kenyan Daily News in 2009 that alluded to the shadow government of the U.S. and the fact that since the election was fixed by having two ineligible candidates who are both under the control of the shadow government, it mattered not who actually "won". The shadow government would still have it's puppet stooge no matter who won. That was and remains a very dangerous and perilous situation. Something that has wounded our nation deeply.

Obama has a plethora of national secrets which, if he were to sell them to the highest bidder, would doom our country. Like Obama, his minion Hillary Clinton has done some dastardly deeds, selling 20% of U.S. uranium to the Russian Federation, abandoning public officials and employees leaving them to their deaths in Benghazi and committing spoliation after illegally downloading Top Secret documents and above onto **a private server,** fixing the DNC Nomination in her favor and generally being a degenerate miscreant.

Obama,Clintons,Biden,the Bushes and McCain are all shadow government figures. The shadow government knew that whoever "won" the 2008 election would be controlled by them, the likes of such people as George Soros or the Bilderbergers. Barack Obama is not eligible to be President. Not only is his Birth Certificate a proven forgery as well as his selective service card, but he has used other people's social security numbers. No one can actually confirm that Obama was born in the manner and under the circumstances that he has proffered.

Obama's biographical narrative is so fraught with inconsis- tencies, so convoluted and misstated, having been changed on numerous occasions, that it is highly suspect and cannot be relied upon. No hospital in Hawaii has claimed that it was the one where the birth of Barack Obama occurred. Sure there were announcements in local newspapers of a "son" being born to Barack Obama and Stanley Dunham. The "son" was not named in the announcement nor was the name of the hospital. Where is the actual Birth Certificate or hospital report?

Foreign operatives and spies have been known to plant people years earlier and to later "announce" them to the public, having every intent of grooming them for a specific goal, like the Presidency. The fact that it has already happened twice proves that he can be done.

There have been various stories published about Obama, one of which was written by reporter Paula Voell of the Buffalo News, on January 20,2009, about a Barbara Nelson of Kenmore, N.Y.

claiming that she had personally spoken to the purported physician that allegedly delivered Barack Obama, Dr. Rodney West and his alleged comments about the name Barack Obama and it's unusual nature. This story was later debunked. Dr. West died in February, 2008 at the age of 98.

Paula Voell was a fellow parishioner of mine at St. Francis of Assisi, R.C. Church in Tonawanda, NY. I spoke to her about the story that she wrote. She stuck to her guns saying it was accurate. It could not have been very accurate given the facts that were uncovered.

One very strange circumstance that occurred is the use of the name "Barbara Nelson" living in Kenmore. It struck me, believe this or not, that my cousin's name was Barbara Nelson and that she had lived in Kenmore, NY. God rest her soul. Was the name "Barbara Nelson" gleened from the Buffalo News obituaries and used by Paula Voell to name a phony witness and to tell a story that never happened"?

Who was this witness named "Barbara Nelson"? Was there really a second person living in Kenmore with the same name as my deceased cousin?

The fact is that the Physician, Rodney West, M.D.,U.S.N. (Ret) having been a Naval Physician, did not deliver civilian babies.

Furthermore, the Physician had left the practice of Medicine in 1956, five years before "Nelson's" claim that said Dr. Rodney West delivered Barack Obama at Kapi'olani Hospital. Navy physicans do not deliver babies at civilian hospitals.

The entire birth narrative of Barack Obama is a fabrication. No one can say with any certainty that Obama was born in one of Hawaii's several Hospitals. Indeed, Earthlink wrote a story years ago stating that not one of Hawaii's hospital claims to be Obama's birthplace. Indeed, several of them adamantly denied it as if it were a blotch on their reputations had their facility been the one where bogus Barry was born.

One would think that all of them would be vying vociferously for the public acknowledgement that a President of the United States had been born at their hospital. In fact, the hospitals in Hawaii were all denying it. They do not want the dubious honor. What does that tell you? It has not been proven that Obama was born in Hawaii and not in Kenya or Indonesia for that matter. Originally, MSNBC's Chris Matthews, reported that Obama was born in Indonesia. Conversely, Obama's purported Kenyan grandmother swore that she was present, in Kenya, at the birth of Barack Obama, Jr. Phony first lady imposter Michelle Obama has also alluded to Barack's birthplace as Kenya as well as Barack Obama himself, broaching the subject of Kenya being his country of origin.

The Kenyan Parliament actually talked, **on record,** about their countryman, Barack Obama, Jr. having attained to the Presidency of the United States. Later, the Kenyan Ambassador was also bragging about Obama's accomplishment saying that Kenya had already erected monuments to Obama.

All of this is a distraction and diversion from what the truth about Obama is, as I have said previously. Purported facts and circumstances of the proffered Obama birth narrative, demonstrate, on it's face, that Obama lied about a lot of things and does not meet constitutional muster and that Obama is a spy, quisling and fraud.

To be President or Vice-President one must be a "Natural Born Citizen". That is "One born in the United States to Parents who are both US Citizens themselves"- Minor v Happersett, USSCt. (1875).

Barack Obama, Sr. was never a U.S. Citizen himself. He could not confer U.S. citizenship on his son if he did not have it himself. By virtue of the fact that Barack Obama, Sr. was a British Subject, he did confer **British citizenship** upon Junior pursuant to the British Nationality Act of 1948. Mere birth in the United States, absent having parents who were both U.S. Citizens, would not help Obama, Jr. He could have been born in the Lincoln bedroom, on T.V., and that wouldn't help him. Birth alone in the U.S. (jus soli) is not enough. A president must also have been born of parents who were both U.S. Citizens themselves (100% jus sanquinis).

Two Americans having a child in the United States begets a 100% "Natural Born [U.S.] Citizen. No one else qualifies as a Natural Born [U.S.] Citizen.

Caveat: If American Citizen parents want their child to be President then they must make sure that they are both American citizens **before** they give birth to their child., and that they have their baby **in** the United States. An NBC **must possess both U.S. jus soli and 100% U.S. jus sanquinis.**

A baby, if born "beyond the seas", off U.S. soil is not a "Natural Born Citizen". Military bases in foreign countries are not U.S. soil. Embassies are not U.S. Soil. Ships, even if owned by U.S. owners are not U.S. soil unless such a ship is in the Harbor of an incorporated U.S. Territory or State, within the 12 mile limit.

In the 2012 election Obama committed his second count of usurpation of the Presidency during war time. Obama has not yet been called on the carpet for his dirty deeds. These days he still walks around freely with seemingly not a care in the world, with that snide smirk on his face which crooked Hillary has adopted and which Bin Laden possessed.

Obama's fellow cabalists, the Clintons, Biden, Bushes and Nancy still remain free. Pelosi is still in Congress and Crooked Hillary Clinton still cons people incessantly along with her lecherous husband Bill "the shill" Clinton. The Clintons, Obama, Biden and the Bushes are all "New World Order" advocates who have spoken in public about it and/or have supported the concept.

George H. W. Bush was the first President that introduced the premise in a speech. His daddy Prescott worked for the man who pushed the idea like a cart through a supermarket, Adolph Hitler. Hitler's plan was for one world government. Prescott Bush was in agreement with Hitler. G.H.W.Bush actually preached it as did G.W.Bush.

Barack Obama in a speech he made in Germany reported by Sky News spoke about "New World Order" and how Obama was a "Citizen of the World". Joe Biden has also supported one world government and the "New World Order". The Clintons are both in sync with the Bushes, Biden and Obama on their plan to usher in a one world government.

Indeed, the U.S. Government printing office publishes a document called "World Governance – 2025". With the Bush's Nazi past and Obama being Muslim, Obama and the Bushes form a modern day Islamo-Nazi concatenation bent on world dominance.

Crooked Hillary has been heard to preach "Open Borders with no walls". That's quintessential "New World Order" stuff. Good news though. The Holy Bible says that New World Order, world governance will fail and also that evil will not prevail against God's Church. That lends comfort to me and it should to all believers in Jesus Christ who is God Incarnate. In these times, the Catholic Church is being attacked from all sides and even from within the halls of the Vatican. Christians in Muslim nations are being killed and are victims of genocide. Yet, the Bible says that as Christians we have nothing to fear. Those who call upon Jesus as their savior will not perish.

Obama is a Muslim supremacist

There is no reward for Muslims who believe in the false god allah. Islam is anathema to freedom. Islam is inextricably linked to Sharia Law. That makes Islam and it's Sharia law "Repugnant to the U.S. Constitution". Contrary to what Barack Obama told us, the United States is not "a Muslim Nation". Down to the last founder, everyone of them believed in God of the Bible. There were a couple of Deists in the group but deists are not atheists.

Strangely, the U.S. Supreme Court has decided that Atheism is a religion, even though atheism,"A-Theism", means absence **of Theism.** Atheists do not believe in God of the Bible. Any "god" is an idol. God is the one and only supreme being.

The important issue is that atheists deny the existence of God of the Bible. Frankly, the U.S. Supreme Court showed themselves fools and geniuses at the same time, for different reasons, when they recognized A-Theism as a religion. As a so called religion atheism cannot now be given **any preference** over other religions. Atheists

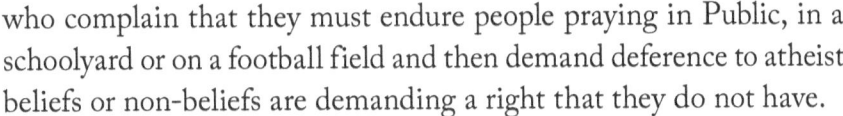

who complain that they must endure people praying in Public, in a schoolyard or on a football field and then demand deference to atheist beliefs or non-beliefs are demanding a right that they do not have.

On the subject of Islam/Sharia Law. The inextricability of Islam with sharia law makes it "Repugnant to the U.S.

Constitution. In Marbury v Madison (1803) the U.S. Supreme court decided that **"ANY law that is repugnant to the U.S. Constitution is null and void".** Islam and atheism are two sides of the same coin. Both deny belief in the one true God, God of the Bible.

It is prohibited for the Government to give deference to one religion in derogation of the rights afforded to other religions. Giving deference to atheism over Christianity would be an unlawful establishment of atheism as the national religion.

Under Obama Islam enjoyed an undue preference and deference in derogation of the establishment clause.

Let me tell you a short story, an anecdote if you may. One day an atheist group sued in Court moving the court to force the government to give them a special holiday called "atheist day".

The presiding Judge in the case told the plaintiffs that they "already have a special holiday for atheists". Querying the Judge on just what date the Judge was alluding to, the Judge answered "April fools day. Anyone who does not believe in God is a fool".

God, of the Bible, the Judge of all Judges actually said it in the Bible: "The fool says in his heart 'there is no God'"-Psalm 14 I believe it was at the 2012 Democratic Convention that the Democrats actually voted to take God entirely out of their platform. The vote was taken several times. The ayes were quite loud. That illustrates the intense aversion that Democrats now have for God. The source of that aversion is Satan. The nays were just as loud. It was a toss up. It was only by the grace of God that the Chair determined that the nays had it.

The Democratic Party of yesteryear has morphed into something unrecognizable as an American party. They have been commandeered over the years by criminal, amoral, anti-American perverted, degenerate, miscreant progressives, communists and liberal bottom feeding scumbags intent on dismantling the moral, ethical and constitutional foundations of the United States of America.

Barack Obama leads that charge against the very fiber and sinew of our nation. He is deeply entrenched in efforts to overthrow the United States and to cause it's demise having very early on stated that he was going to "Change the very foundations of America". His faux "administration" was a Racketeer Influenced Corrupt Organization. The remnants of it continues to this day to act, in concert with other anti-Americans, in derogation of the U.S. Constitution. Barack Obama belongs in the Brig. Barack Obama stands accused of Treason by the requisite (2) witnesses to the same overt act of treason, mandated by the U.S. Constitution, See:

Article III, Sec. 3, Clause 1, USConst. I am the second of those witnesses. Obama stands accused of Treason by the first witness to have accused him of treason, Lt. Cmdr. Walter Fitzpatrick,III, USN, (Ret.).

When I say Obama stands accused I mean that over the last (9) years several formal charges have been lodged against him with the FBI, Secret Service, ICE, Congress, former AG of the US Eric Holder, the DC Police, the Tonawanda Police, the Department of Defense, Provost Marshals and very recently with the Chairman, Joint Chiefs of Staff Dunford, AG of the US Jeff Sessions and President Trump, inter alia.

In 2012, Barack Obama was given written notice and formally served legal notice through then U.S. Attorney Eric Holder, that Obama had been placed under formal citizen's arrest for usurpation of the Presidency during war time. This writer was the arresting party. The powers that be at the time were seriously, and I mean criminally nonfeasant. All the numerous citizen's complaints, charges, lawsuits, exposes, news stories, radio and newspaper interviews have led to a solidly anchored government stonewall.

I suspect that the Central Intelligence Agency had their hand in the 2008 and 2012 presidential elections. Obama once served as an interpreter of arabic in the Soviet-Afghan war. I wouldn't put it pass the CIA to try and wrench control of the government from the legitimate powers that be. Lee Harvey Oswald worked for the CIA. Not widely publicized was the recent placement of a memorial star **in Oswald's memory** on the memorial wall of HQ of the Central Intelligence Agency.

In the 2008 election both the Republicans and the Democrats proffered constitutionally barred candidates to be President. As explained earlier in this tome, neither John McCain or Barack Obama are "Natural Born Citizens" of the United States.

Let me tell you another short story, an anecdote, if you may. Obama once claimed that his "Uncle helped liberate Auschwitz in WWII". The issue with that is that it was the Red Army, Russians, that liberated Auschwitz. So, was Obama saying that his "Uncle" fought in WWII in the Russian Army?

Is Barack Obama a Russian double agent having served in the Soviet-Aghanistan War as an interpreter for the CIA while spying for the soviets? Think Lee Harvey Oswald when you think about how conniving the CIA can be.

Lee Harvey Oswald was recently and quietly honored with a star on the memorial wall at CIA HQ. A large pile of records of that assassination have been released as of October 26, 2017, by Executive order of President Trump.

Barack Obama is a mystery man. His birth narrative and life narrative are extremely suspect and the narratives and facts of his biography have vacillated Machiavellianistically given Obama's contemporaneous circumstances. Obama changed his bio several times and has used such changes it to his advantage. Obama is a master Muslim taqyist., a Liar of the highest order.

Obama went out of his way to facilitate the immigration of Muslims into the United States and the enactment of special provisions in the Affordable care act that cater to Muslims, he has held Ramadan Iftars in the White House and has publicly said that he "supports Zakat".

Zakat is the so called Islamic "Charity" and is actually a mandatory tax that all Muslims must pay, the funds of which are distributed **only** to Muslim causes. Very noteworthy is that a full 1/8ᵗʰ of all Zakat goes to support America's enemies, the **Islamic Military.** Obama went on several trips outside the U.S. all the time apologizing for America's purported colonialism and imperialism. He has cancelled Christian Days of Prayer, covered up Christian Sacramentals at Catholic colleges that he spoke at and he wears a gold ring that says "alahu akbar" on it. Obama speaks fluent arabic.

Notre Dame's "Doctor" of Death

Obama is Notre Dame's "Doctor" of Death. A staunch pro-abortion proponent, Obama even denied medical care to the survivors of "Botched" abortions. He voted "present" when the vote was called. How can any catholic university give an honorary degree to such a degenerate bottom feeder?

Obama has given billions of American Taxpayer funds to our enemies, he has made deals with Iran that have helped Iran and have not curtailed their nuclear aspirations.

Obama traded five high level Muslim warlords for a U.S. Army deserter named Bowe Bergdahl. People that should still be alive, died on his watch looking for him after he absconded from his post. Bergdahl got a demotion to Private from Sergeant, a Dishonorable discharge and a $10,000 fine.

Several of the soldiers who were ordered to go out and look for Bergdahl **lost their lives or were injured.**

It doesn't ever stop Bogus Barry Obama and one of his cabalists, Crooked Hillary were responsible for the death of four Americans in Benghazi. This was a crime for which Obama and Clinton suffered no repercussion. These are only some examples of why I know that Obama is a Muslim supremacist, usurper, traitor and spy.

I served in the U.S. Navy in the 1970's. I had a "Secret" Clearance that started at the "Confidential" level. If I, or any of my shipmates who had clearances, were to divulge just a miniscule or diminutive fragment of the classified information that I was entrusted with to anyone who was not cleared, I would have been sent to the brig. In fact, one of my shipmates was court-martialed for disclosing information. Have those laws against espionage changed? I think not.

What has changed is that the powers that be were so corrupt in the RICO "administration" of Bogus Barry that extremely criminal activity was engaged in and was then subsequently ignored, with impunity. Barack Obama and Hillary Clinton committed Espionage and Treason. Crooked Hillary then engaged in spoliation of the massive amounts of evidence. That makes Hillary Clinton a traitor and a spy. Her husband Bill Clinton,either conspired with the DOJ and/or threatened them if they went after crooked Hillary.

Our ex-Presidents are given too much deference. They are no longer President and should not be called "President". In fact, Obama never was President, for even one second. We have been in a time of war for at least the last (15) years. The U.S. was declared a war zone by Obama several years ago. That makes Obama's usurpation of the Presidency, during war time, an act of treason & espionage and it makes Obama a traitor and a spy. Those are capital offenses carrying the death penalty, if convicted. I believe that a military firing squad is warranted for Barack Obama, Jr. if he is ever convicted.

Hillary Clinton should be in prison facing the death penalty for her crimes. "If I were President, you would be in Jail"- said candidate Donald J. Trump, Sr. now President Trump, to Hillary Clinton during a Presidential debate.

Hillary believes that it was her "turn" to be President but it doesn't work that way.

One must be elected by the American People. Hillary was significantly rejected by the voters in 2016. Hillary Clinton would have been a pox on the United States had she been elected. There is no way that she should have even been allowed to reach the point where she became the opposing candidate against then candidate Donald J. Trump, Sr. She is a felon.

Compared to Barack Obama who is a degenerate, criminal, miscreant Hillary Clinton is even more corrupt. To be more corrupt then Barack Obama is a very dubious accomplishment because one would have to have standards that are so debase that it would make someone like Rosemary West blush.

Obama is a wannabe world dictator Pol Pot class. Obama is amoral as is Hillary Clinton. Neither seem like they possess moral compasses. If they do, they keep them well out of sight.

At least the Presidential election of 2016 was between two constitutionally eligible U.S. Citizens. Both Clinton and Trump are "Natural Born Citizens". To reiterate, neither Barack Obama or John McCain are "Natural Born Citizens". That means that the fix was in in the 2008 and 2012 Presidential election.

In 2008, Obama co-conspirator Nancy Pelosi made false reports to Election officials, when she affirmed to the State of Hawaii that Obama met all Article II, criteria. Of course, he does not. With regard to the other (49) States Pelosi deleted the paragraph that appeared on the form which had to be sworn to, attesting that Obama met all criteria. Pelosi committed fraud.

Furthermore, Pelosi created a diversion at the time at which, after the counting of the electoral votes, Vice President Cheney was supposed to ask "Are there any objections"? Normally, if an elector wishes to object to anything about that count, he can. There is a point in the process in which the Vice-President is to ask the electors "Are there any Objections to the count". In the Obama election that responsibility fell on Vice-President Cheney. At the precise instance where the question "are there any objections to the count", was supposed to be asked, Nancy Pelosi started clapping and cheering causing others to do so. Vice-President Cheney never got to ask the question. This can be confirmed by watching the proceedings on youtube. I've seen it. Cheney did not ask the question "are there any objections to the count"?

Later, the media reported that there were "No objections".

Fact is, Objections were not entertained. Several electors later said that they **had objections** but they were not given the floor.

So, what can be done about this chicanery by an ordinary, everyday citizen? Well, let me tell you. I looked into it. By trial and error I went about contacting the powers that be, writing letters to editors of newspapers, approaching TV and Radio personalities and filing legal challenges with my State Board of Elections. I participated in two Citizen's Grand Juries on this issue, I sued Obama in the Courts of New York State and at the U.S. Supreme Court. For the last (9) years I have written blogs on Topix and have used Twitter and Facebook to get my story across to the nation.

I've written in various newspapers such as Pravda, Le Monde, Joop, Der Spiegel, Australia Today, the Post and Email, the Potterville Post, the Buffalo News and the Tonawanda News. I was once interviewed by the (3) major news network affiliates in Buffalo, New York.,NBC and CBS and ABC. They, all (3) of them, stifled the story after the interview. What got to me is that even Fox news which is normally very conscientious in reporting the facts, turned against "Birthers". It could have something to do with the fact that Muslims own part of Fox.

Birthers are everyday people making a living like everyone else. They are more American then others however. They actually care if the Constitution is adhered to or not. It could not be plainer. The founders did not want foreign influence to insinuate itself into the workings of our government. That happened too many times in the monarchies of the world when perhaps a Spanish King would marry a French Queen and thus double the power parameters of their Kingdoms.

Foreign influence in our US Government would be and is proscribed in the U.S. Constitution. American public officials aren't even allowed to take gifts from a foreign nation without declaring them. Foreign influence is taboo. The US Constitution does not allow the use of any title of nobility. I have qualms about the U.S. Government calling certain of their unelected officials "Czars". That is unconstitutional. Given that "Lady" is also a title of Nobility, should we be giving the wife of a President such deference as to call her First "Lady"? On this I must point out that "First Lady" is not a public office and has never been one. That said, Melania is more of a Lady, and a classy lady at that, then Michelle Obama was. Indeed, Michelle Obama may not be a lady at all. Interpret that as you will. Obama, on occasion, had referred to him/her as "Michael" several times.

Presidents must be "Natural Born Citizens"

It was with great logic and rationale that our first Chief Justice of the Supreme Court, John Jay, recommended the prohibition that none but a "Natural Born Citizen" be President. Fox news commentators like Bill O'Reilly called birthers "pinheads". Birthers are not "Pinheads". I am not a "pinhead". I have researched this matter diligently for (9) years now. Sheppard Smith, Glen Beck and even Sean Hannity disparaged birthers. **Fox news!**

They are supposed to be the bastian of conservative thought and news reporting. To this day no one on Fox will stand up for what is right and speak the truth about the Obama usurpation. Perhaps it is the Fox news staff that are intellectually encumbered. Perhaps it is censorship. Fox News is partially owned by Muslims and has offices in Dubai, UAE. They were most likely stifled by political correctness or stifled from disparaging the Muslim supremacist and usurper in the White House at the time.

In other words they became Dhimmis which are non-muslims leading a restricted life under control of Islam. Remember what I said about the significance of Dubai? As for other cable news and mainstream media, the majority couldn't care less that a person, with a dubious and hidden birth and life narr-ative, usurped the Presidency during time of war.

What patriotic American would do such a thing? They wouldn't. Only anti-American progressive liberals, communists, socialists and other miscreants that roam the Earth would side with Barack Obama who is a quisling and a spy.

Many of the proactive steps that I have taken were stonewalled by the powers that be. The shadow government is, to this day, so corrupt, that they continue to allow a treasonous scoundrel like Barack Obama, who usurped the Presidency during war time, to walk about freely and unscathed by his criminal activities and chicanery. He plans to make a quick exit if he has to. You may not be aware of it but Obama has a house in Dubai, UAE. Dubai has no extradition treaty with the United States.

I conjecture that Obama plans to escape to the UAE when and if the "Political winds turn ugly".,that he will flee the United States. Obama will make his move soon. You can count on it. The Trump DOJ and Congressional Investigations are starting to go after the Clintons. They should be investigating Obama. Obama and his cabal are traitors and spies.

Extensive evidence against the Clintons, Loretta Lynch, Comey and Obama regarding Hillary's acts of espionage using a private server as well as her Russian Uranium deal and Benghazi scandal will lead to members of the Obama cabal having to find the closest exit available to leave the United States.

Sometimes Justice is slower then a broken clock but twice a day the time is right. The time is right now for the legal authorities to stop being lily-livered and to arrest Obama and several members of his RICO cabal. They have had scores of opportunities in the past (9) years to bring Obama to justice.

For the last several months the left has been attempting to assassinate President Trump's character. Several degenerates in Hollywood and in Congress have even threatened physical assassination. That is atrocious and must not be tolerated. It is a felony under 18USC, Sec.871(a).

The Obama cabalists have used fake news, fraud, hyperbole, exaggeration, paid protestors, corrupt public officials, paid newscasters and otherwise shady and seedy agents in order to attempt to reject the fair and legal election of President Trump, a 100% "Natural Born [American] Citizen" born in the U.S. to parents who were both U.S. Citizens themselves.

President Trump is an authentic, bona-fide, legally elected real President. The left hates that fact. Crooked Hillary wanted to open our borders wide, to let anyone that wanted in to come here, without **any** vetting. She does not want border walls she wants the border police to stand down. Hillary Clinton is quite unstable. What amount of money slaked her greed enough to disseminate national secrets and to betray the United State to such an extent that people are calling for her arrest and imprisonment?

Why would anyone want such a nasty woman like crooked Hillary, a woman that would make infamous criminal Elizabeth Bathory blush, to be President of the United States? That would be tantamount to electing Charles Manson. On second thought, he could end up to be the better choice. That doesn't say much for Hillary. People disappear when the Clintons are around. Not unlike, Elizabeth Bathory, Crooked Hillary's social status seems to have saved her, for a time. from being imprisoned and that is simply unconstitutional.

No one should be above the law. It used to be "No one is above the law". But apparently there are some people who are.

Former DNC Chairwoman, Donna Brazile says that she has found proof that the DNC rigged the Democratic nomination in favor of Hillary Clinton. Bernie Sanders should be perturbed. Can you say "Super Delegates"? Hillary stacked the deck.

Hillary, being the devout Obama cabalist that she is copies many of Bogus Barry's tactics. The Obama "administration" acted to "visit" those of us who filed complaints. His Courts charged some of us who sued with having filed frivolous cases, fined some of us and arrested others. Obama's RICO regime made the old time Mafiosi look amateurish. There's definitely a double standard operating in the U.S. Government.

America was under siege for (8) years from November, 2008 until January 20, 2017 by an imposter in the oval office impersonating a President. We had no real President from Jan. 2009 until Jan. 2017. See: "There is no 'President' Obama" which can be viewed in the archives of the online newspaper the Post and Email. Biden was never the bona-fide Vice President either. For a time both Boehner and Ryan were in the position to attain the Presidency. They both served as Speaker of the House at one time while Obama was usurping the office of the Presidency and were both.at one time, in line of succession to attain to the Presidency had only law enforcement not been nonfeasant and did their duty to arrest Obama.

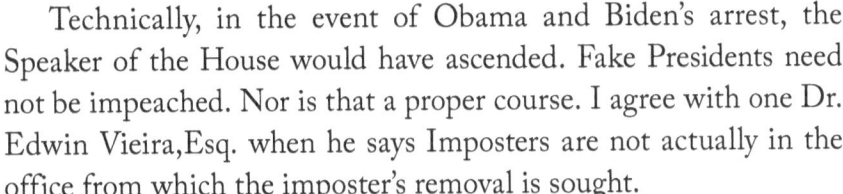

Technically, in the event of Obama and Biden's arrest, the Speaker of the House would have ascended. Fake Presidents need not be impeached. Nor is that a proper course. I agree with one Dr. Edwin Vieira,Esq. when he says Imposters are not actually in the office from which the imposter's removal is sought.

Barack Obama is a shadow government puppet. He is being controlled by the dark State which envelops all aspects of life in the United States these days. This, eerily is the same manner Islam/ Sharia Law operates. It encroaches and infringes on every aspect of life in Muslim countries. Obama is intent on making the United States the "Muslim nation" that he claimed it already was. I will go into more detail later. How does a constitutionally barred candidate who does not meet Article II muster get "elected" to be President of the United States? How is it that Barack Obama was actually allowed to perpetrate such a treasonous scheme and to effectuate a faux "administration" which operated unscathed for (8) years? It's similar to the question that must have been asked by some people in 1930s Germany. How does a low life German Army Corporal usurp an entire government to become it's ersatz leader?

These pseudo leaders had help doing so. Bogus Barry managed to usurp the Presidency of the United States by fraudulent means. He was a spurious illegal and phony "President". One person that helped him get there was Nancy Pelosi as I had explained earlier. She perjured herself in order to allow Obama to perpetrate his heinous scam against "We the People".

Obama was assisted by his attorneys at Perkins-Coie. They actually were paid by Obama to "find a way to circumvent Article II". Obama paid them hundreds of thousands of dollars.

If anything, Perkins-Coie has violated ABA ethical conduct standards. Perkins-Coie is complicit with Obama's usurpation.

The arabs helped Obama. Obama was groomed by the arabs to infiltrate the Presidency and then to work toward advancing Palestinian and Islamic causes, quid pro quo.

Obama usurped the Presidency,by fraud, in a time of war. That's a capital offense and like a trusted mafia consigliare, Perkins-Coie helped Obama do the dirty deed. Joe Biden should not go unscathed either. Biden, as Obama's so called "Vice-President" was also without legal bona-fides. Since Obama was not the bona-fide POTUS, that made Joe Biden an imposter too. Obama had no legal authority to name anyone to be his Vice-President. Joe Biden is having rumblings of running for POTUS in 2020. That is not in the interests of the United States. Bogus Biden is as bogus as bogus Barry.

Say that (3) times fast.

It was a disgracefully scandalous masquerade that was palmed off on the naïve American voters who voted for Obama. It is a scam foisted upon the United States by a criminal, degenerate miscreant con man named Obama.

Where was Homeland Security when all this was going on?

It wasn't as if they knew nothing about it. Had Hillary Clinton won the 2016 election she would have shoved everything under the proverbial rug and she would have pardoned Barack Obama when and if he ever gets tried and convicted. What kind of government allows such a large presence of criminal activities and corruption perpetrated from within, to go on unabated for years?

Congress and the several Law Enforcement organizations in the United States continuously investigate the likes of people like Hillary Clinton. The many formal complaints filed against Obama probably never were investigated.

Day in and day out, congress engages in perfunctory half-hearted and habitual senate and congressional committee hearings. They very rarely, if ever, seem to reach any actual conclusions assigning blame to anyone, sending anything to a Federal Grand Jury or making any arrests. Instead, endless investigations are done, hundreds of questions are asked, endless requests under the Freedom of Information Act are made that are infrequently honored or documents are released that are so extensively redacted that the documents are rendered nugatory and useless. I have seen documents with entire pages blacked out. That is **not** in keeping with the spirit of the Freedom of Information Act.

I doubt seriously that this was the original congressional intent of the FOIA. A contemporaneous example is the recent redaction of certain parts of the files regarding the assass-ination of John F. Kennedy. The files were supposed to be released after "fifty years". When Kennedy was murdered, in 1963, the FOIA didn't even exist. It was the government that decided that the files would be kept from the public for "fifty years".

That time has elapsed. With regard to all of the Committee hearings in Congress, into such matters as Benghazi, Uranium One,Hillary Clinton's acts of Espionage, Lynch's and Comey's nonfeasance,etc., I want to know. When is anyone actually going to go to prison?

Investigation of serious crimes is only part of the process by which criminals are brought to the bar of Justice. Holding repetitive continuous hearings and going no further doesn't meet muster. We the People must demand more. People should be going to jail. The United States is not supposed to be a place where crimes are dismissed on a mere apology,where it's elites are above the law and given illegal deference.

Where was Homeland Security from 2008 until 2017? Where were the miltary provost marshalls?

Barack Obama usurped the Presidency during time of war and has so far not suffered any repercussions for doing so.

That he usurped the Presidency during wartime makes Obama a spy under 10USC, Sec. 906, Art.106. He is a spy and a quisling. Hillary Clinton, is a member of his cabal and part of what Dr. Richard Boylan calls "The Geoplutocratic 'elite' bent on Global domination". BHO and HRC are both New World Order advocates, as are the Bushes,Biden and Bill.

We are a country in which everyone is born equal. There should be no special treatment to so called "elites". The U.S. should not have citizens that are treated as "elites". Justice should be meted out as fairly and equitably to the homeless person, with his legal aid attorney, as it is to such as Hillary Clinton and Barack Obama with their inextricably attached teams of legal eagles.

Lawyers like Perkins-Coie, who are unethically helping them find ways to legally evade the constitution should be disbarred.

Others, are researching ways how to defraud the American taxpayer in ways that would embarrass the scummiest "gansta" con men.

Did you know that Obama and Michelle were both disbarred as Lawyers? The Obamas are both degenerate miscreants.

Obama is a person of interest and perhaps a suspect in the Trinity United Church of Christ murders. The Pastor, Reverend Jeremiah "God damn America" Wright introduced Barack Obama to Michelle Obama. Wright was one of the people homosexual men would seek out when they needed a "Beard". A "beard" is a woman who is linked up, for the sake of appearances, with a gay man in order for the gay man to appear to be a married, heterosexual man.

Ten years ago, in November, 2007, Donald Young, Larry Bland and Nate Spencer were murdered, execution style. The three were all homosexual church members in the church which Obama went to for (20) years. Donald Young was the Choir Director and it has been said that he and Barack Obama were intimate.

Obama is gay. He also has a history of smoking crack. He was intimate with one of his Secret Service entourage named Reggie Love, his Secret Service "Body Man". Barack Obama is a man of very low moral standards, a degenerate miscreant who promoted late term abortions and the denial of medical care to survivors of botch abortions. Obama and Rahm Emmanuel belonged to the same gay health club in Chicago.

Obama is evil. From where does such evil emanate? If one believes in God then one has to believe in Satan. Obama is not a Christian. Nor is he a Jew. Obama is a muslim. I believe as Peter Hammond does that Islam is not a religion and that Islam is Satanic. Such persons as Salmon Rushdie who wrote "The Satanic verses" and Dr. Peter Hammond who wrote "Slavery, Terrorism and Islam" back me up.

Conjectures of Barack Obama possibly being related to or associated with Adolph Hitler in some way.

My next topic will be a discussion of familial traits and how connecting the dots has led to the conjecture, by some, that Obama could actually be the son of Adolph Hitler. The significance of the possibility that Obama's was spawned by Hitler or had close familial ties to Hitler is flabbergasting. It boggles the mind. There is a book called "The Death of Hitler". It is reported in the book that Hitler fled to Indonesia and lived there, posing as a Doctor named George Poch. In one of the reviews of the book a person made a comment saying that one of the people in a picture with Poch "Looks like the U.S. President Barack Obama". I have frequently conjectured that Obama is Indonesian and not Caucasian-Negroid.

Obama lived in Indonesia as did Hitler. Obama's purported Mother, Stanley Dunham was a member of a cult called Subud, as was Loretta Fuddy of the Hawaii Department of Vital Stats. Subud is headquartered in Indonesia. Stranger things have happened in History, but these conjectures and theories are intriguing.

In an ideal world we the people would not have to conjecture about who the hell "Barack Obama" really is. His COLB is a forgery so conjecture as to who he really is, is all we can have.

All manner of vetting should have been done by someone at every step in the process of his attaining to the Presidency of the United States. He should not have been allowed to become President until he proved who he was and until he proffered all the certified documents necessary to prove his identity. McCain also slipped through the same cracks. Neither of the two are eligible to be President of the United States of America under Article II of the U.S. Constitution.

Some critics of those of us who want the truth say that there would have to be too many people involved to pull off such a huge scam and they then ask if we "Birthers" are accusing everyone in the government? We may very well have to. A quisling usurper made his way into the Oval Office with such impunity and ease, that he has to have had significant help from others. Those others are our nations domestic and foreign enemies.

The incontrovertible fact is that Barack Obama's true identity cannot be ascertained given the documents that he has hence proffered. His birth narrative and life biography are so chock full of inconsistencies that his real identity has not been and may not be confirmed for years. I know that Obama is not who he claims to be. Someone planted this guy, insinuating him into American life, the way the Soviets did in the fifties when they would have whole families set up shop as Americans. Whole families would be trained how to blend in, speak our language, go to our schools, live and work here. Kids, Adults even their pets were all Soviet plants. I go far enough back to remember when Nikita Sergeyevich Khrushchev, First Secretary of the Soviet Communist Party acted out at the Polish Embassy in Moscow in November,1956 when he told the United States "Whether you like it or not history is on our side" and that the U.S.S.R. "will bury" the U.S.

Some have said that he meant that he would destroy the U.S and others have said that he meant only that the U.S.S.R. would outlive the United States which as history has shown did not occur.

The U.S.S.R. is no longer in existence. However, that is not stopping Vladimir Putin from trying to resurrect or recon-stitute the U.S.S.R. or something similar, from his Kremlin digs in Moscow.

In 1960 Khrushchev had one of his childish temper tantrums at the U.N. when he started banging his shoe on the desk like a gavel. I was nine years old when that happened. Khrushchev was a hellion., an overgrown soviet brat. Putin who is ex KGB is much more reserved.

The faux Obama "administration" was steeped in cloak and dagger clandestine subterfuge. Obama was giving millions if not billions of American taxpayer's money to the enemy. He early on in his "term" gave millions to Palestinians. Later on in it he gave billions to Iran in an extremely bad deal with them regarding their development of nuclear capabilities.

Obama support's Islamic "Zakat". Zakat is a so called Islamic "Charity" but every muslim has an obligation to pay it. It is not voluntary. "I want to help every Muslim fulfill his religious **obligation** of zakat. I support Zakat" said Barack Obama. It would be easy for the reader to do his own research on Zakat.

A full 1/7th of which is **dedicated to be paid to the Islamic military. Our enemies.**

While Obama was impersonating a public official, acting as President without legal authority or bona-fides, trillions of dollars disappeared from the U.S. Treasury. That's with a "T".

The miscreant had U.S. taxpayers supporting the enemy right under our noses. The more Muslim taxpayers that we allow to enter and work here the more money is paid to the "Islamic military". The immigration of Muslims within our borders serves the Jihadi Hijrah. Obama has schemed to bring about the collapse of the U.S. Government.

Obama helped introduce sharia law in Kenya with his "paternal cousin" Raila Odinga. Obama wants sharia in the U.S.

Raila Oding ran against an ally of the United States, Mwai Kibacki, President of Kenya. Kibacki is a Catholic. Odinga is a Muslim as is Obama. Odinga has close ties to and is associated with the Islamic terrorists who bombed the U.S. Embassies in Dar es Salaam, Tanzania and in Nairobi, Kenya in 1998.

The turncoat Barack Obama went so far as to actively campaign for Raila Odinga, in Kenya, while Obama was a U.S. Senator. I don't believe that activity jibes with the Logan Act, 18USC, Sec. 953. It doesn't. In ex-officio, Obama recently met with Justin Trudeau regarding U.S. foreign policy. Obama is at it again. He is no longer a public official. He is interfering with the Trump administration and the undermining the United States. Violating the Logan Act is a felony.

What kind of American, while a U.S. Senator no less, engages in activities such as campaigning for an enemy of the United States., an opponent of our allies, undermining U.S. interests, getting involved in the government of a foreign nation while owing allegiance to the United States of America? What kind of American? A treasonous one like Barack Obama.

Barack Obama and Raila Odinga even had the **same** campaign slogan "**CHANGE**'.

Did I mention that Obama was recently called up for Jury duty in Chicago? He was excused and sent home. In any event, any attorney worth his sheepskin would emphatically squelch, and challenge in voir dire, having Obama serve on any jury that would be deciding the evidence against any client of theirs. Obama is a picaroon, a degenerate rogue, a scoundrel and a miscreant. He is a free man with a prison cell in his future.

One reason that he is not in jail is because he had the power of the Presidency at his fingertips, albeit illicitly obtained, to keep himself out of the brig. There is hope that the Trump administration will do something constructive in the pursuit of justice against Obama and perhaps proactively order that Obama be arrested by the Military Provost Marshall for usurpation of the Presidency during wartime. A UCMJ offense punishable by death. It was wartime then in 2008 and 2012 when Obama usurped the Presidency and it is still wartime now in 2017. Because it was wartime when bogus Barry Obama committed usurpation of the Presidency of the United States, Obama violated the Espionage provisions of 10USC, the Uniform Code of Military Justice referring to being a spy. See: 10USC, Sec. 906, Art. 106.

Should Obama be able to walk about freely for the rest of his life, unscathed by the heinous crimes he has committed against the United States of America and We the people? I think not. Most if not all of leftist progressives will disagree. The crimes of espionage during war time is a capital offense. It is very serious even when committed outside of war. But we have been at war for 15 years or more, at this writing.

Such crimes as treason and espionage carry the death penalty.

Bogus Barry had eight years in the White House in which to carry out his sinister plans to "change the very foundation of America". The election of Donald J. Trump, Sr. dashed any further plans that he could actively facilitate. Eight full years with Obama in possession of the nuclear football, all of the nation's secrets, the key to the federal treasury, access to congress and the senate, being in charge of foreign affairs, Obama had unlawful control of the strongest nation on Earth.

If it were not for the 24/7 scrutiny that we "Birthers" placed on Obama and if he thought that he was not being watched, the

United States might not be here today. Hillary Clinton would have constituted a third Obama term. Birther efforts slowed down Obama's sinister plans. Birthers are to be commended.

Obama even had control of the very people who should have put the kibosh on Obama's plan to overthrow our Government by fraud, Homeland Security. Where was Homeland Security on January 20, 2009 when Obama illegally entered into the Office of the Presidency of the United States of America? They were nonfeasant for a second time on January 20,2013 when Obama committed his second count of usurpation of the presidency of the United States, by fraud.

Where were the Judges? Many lawsuits ensued against Obama. A large number of Judges before whom cases against Obama came, dropped the cases, on technicalities, or by claiming that they were frivolous cases. Some persons were actually sanctioned by the courts for pursuing their right to petition the government for redress of wrongs. Many of the Judges stated that the Plaintiffs had "no standing". One of the plaintiffs is an actual former candidate for President, Cody Robert Judy. I too at one time "threw my hat into the ring".

See: "Robert Laity for President" on google.

The malfeasant actions of these nonfeasant Judges didn't faze some of those plaintiffs. They stood their grounds and they fought the overt corruption. There are calls for justice to high heaven over Obama's usurpation of the Presidency. Something stinks in D.C. One of my favorite sayings is "Don't give up the ship" it was uttered by James Lawrence, the Captain of the U.S.S. Chesapeake during the war of 1812.

In the same vein, we must not give up America to supplanters and usurpers. Obama is immutably an imposter. I would hazard to say that it is very well known and widely believed that this is the case. There is a humongous "elephant in the room" and it's colored Red for communist. The Communist Party of America endorsed both Barack Obama for President in 2012 and Hillary Clinton for President in 2016.

The Democratic Party is not my father and mother's democratic party. Nor is it the one I used to belong to, before they decided to scam we the people by proffering a constitutionally barred candidate to be President. Recently, it has surfaced that the Democrat party stacked the deck in the 2016 election, setting up the nomination for Hillary Clinton.

This was confirmed by former DNC Chairwoman Donna Brazile. The CPUSA recently protested the DNC's comman-deering of their platform.

In 2008 I became a Republican after being a life long Democrat. I voted for McCain. I found out later that, he too, is constitutionally barred from being President because he too is not a "Natural Born Citizen" of the United States. Saints preserve us. Now what? Both parties are in on it? Yes.

Both parties are in on the scam to install a person in the oval office that is not an Article II "Natural Born Citizen". The reason being that a foreigner would be more malleable to the whims of the likes of the Bilderbergers, Trilateral Commission, Foreign Relations Committee, Communists, Rothschilds, George Soros and the former Presidents.

Like putty in the hands of someone, Obama was and is a puppet of the shadow government. He is Rotten to the core.

Note: A year has passed since Donald J. Trump, Sr, was legally elected to be our U.S. President. Since "President #21" and "President #43" were both phony, President Trump is actually President #43 and not "President #45".

Obama illegally flies the Chinese flag over the South Lawn of the White House on the Republic of China's 60th Anniversary

President Trump recently finished a 12 day visit to Asia and was in Bejing, China and several other Asian countries. The Chinese government flew the American Flag in Bejing while he was there. When a head of State is present, the proper flag protocol is to fly their nation's flag, the flag of the United States in this case because President Trump, was present at the time.

What authority did Barack Obama have to raise the Communist Red Flag of the People's Republic of China, on the South Lawn of the White House and to celebrate the 60th anniversary of it's inception in 2009? None!

That was a clear violation of law considering the fact that the Chinese head of State at his home in China at the time. I am asking why the United States Government celebrated **any** anniversary of the People's Republic of Chinese using American taxpayer funds?

That Obama had no qualms about honoring the communist republic, under which millions of people die under tyrannical rule, was a clear indication that Barack Obama identifies with communism and has diminished or no loyalty to the United States of America and that he has minimal if any interest in the protests and sentiments of the countless Americans who were against such a celebration of communism. I doubt very seriously that Chinese officials would fly the Stars and Stripes over Jianfu Palace on the 4th of July if the President of the United States wasn't actually visiting at the time.

Many of those of us who fought in combat against the Chinese in Korea and in Vietnam were disgusted with Barack Obama's deference to China to the detriment of the United States. It was atrocious and unconscionable behavior by Obama.

While our current President Trump put's "America first", Bogus Barry Obama placed the United States last. When Obama went on overseas trips Obama would incessantly apologize for what he called the arrogance, dismissiveness, and dictatorial aspects of the United States. Instead of holding up America's light to the world, Obama accused the U.S. of having a "Darker" side. Obama is just projecting his traits on others.

Obama is nothing like President Trump who holds America in high esteem and hold's it's light high to the world. President Trump is a "good cheerleader for America" as his son, Donald, Jr. once said that he would be.

Obama hates America and White People

Obama hates America. Obama is a racist Muslim Supremacist.

Obama, Sr. was a Muslim. His purported Mother Stanley Dunham was White. Obama once said that he hated his Mother's race and that hate had not gone away. At the time Dunham "married" Obama,Sr., Jr.'s purported Father, Senior was married to a woman named Kezia in Kenya. Senior was a polygamist. Dunham had been pregnant for (3) months prior to marrying Obama, Sr. Again, all of Obama's birth narrative is suspect given the fact that his birth certificate is a proven and documented forgery. Obama had the nerve to say that the United States was "dark". Obama is a machiavellian, prevaricating, mendacious, lying, master muslim taqyyist. If he tells you that the sky is blue. Don't believe him. Muslims are raised to lie for their so called "faith" if it advances Islam.

We the People must be extremely careful about Islam in our midst. Islam is anathema. We were warned in the past, by several founding fathers, including Thomas Jefferson. You might ask then, why did Thomas Jefferson own a Q'uran? He owned it so that he could learn more about how our nation's **enemies** thought. I own one for that same reason. Barack Obama, after he purposely flubbed the oath which presidents are required to take to enter office forewent taking the oath on a Bible eschewing the Bible, He then went inside and reportedly swore an oath on Jefferson's Q'uran in private.

Obama foresworn himself, thereby committing perjury, by having taken **any** oath of office to become President, whether on a Bible or a Q'uran. Obama is not now, nor was he ever eligible to be President of the United States pursuant to Article II of the U.S. Constitution.

Justice of the U.S. Supreme Court, Clarence Thomas in 2009 told then Congressman Jose Serrano that the U.S. Supreme Court was **"evading the Obama eligibility issue".** That nonfeasant answer to Serrano resulted in raucous laughter in the committee hearing in which Thomas said it. Shame on all of them at that congressional hearing. It certainly is not a laughing matter to have a SCOTUS

Justice admit in public that the U.S. Supreme Court Justices are "evading" a constitutional issue that it is their sworn duty to reconcile.

In any event, it is extremely noteworthy that Justice Clarence Thomas, et al's predecessors on the Court had not evaded that very same issue (134) years earlier in 1875 when the entire (9) then Justices of the U.S. Supreme Court **unanimously** established that a "Natural Born Citizen" is one that is born in the United States of parents who are both U.S. Citizens themselves. It is because of nonfeasant, malfeasant and misfeasant Judges and public officials that "We the People" had to endure, and were subjected to the rule of, an ineligible disqualified and constitutionally barred, counterfeit "President" from 2009 until 2017.

Obama should have been and could have been arrested on the spot and prosecuted in the U.S. District Court in D.C. or alternatively, Court-Martialed by the military for espionage during wartime under 10USC, Sec.906, Art. 106.

To begin with, It is important to note that prosecuting Obama by Impeachment would have been totally inappropriate and improper given the fact that Obama was never actually the bona-fide President. Obama was never in the position from which his removal was being sought.

Any claim that he had any kind of executive privilege from arrest as a sitting President was groundless and fallacious since he was never a sitting President. Obama is barred from being President due to not meeting constitutional standards and criteria in Article II. In any event, there is precedent in arresting even a sitting President. President U.S. Grant, while in office, was taken into custody by the D.C. Police for speeding in his horse drawn carriage.

There is also U.S. Supreme Court precedent that states that a sitting president is **not immune** from prosecution for acts committed before he took office. See: **Clinton v. Jones, USSCt.**

Insofar as Obama was actually not in office legally, he was but a de facto phony "president" and never a de jure President.

U.S. District Court, Western District of New York Magistrates Schroeder and Foschio instructed me to file my criminal complaint against Obama in D.C. with Local Law enforcement. That is where the usurpation of the Presidency occurred. The two imposters in the Oval Office that I mentioned, Obama and Arthur were never actually President.

Any legally authorized D.C. law enforcement official could have walked in to the White House with an arrest warrant for Obama issued by a U.S. District Court Justice, District of D.C.

According to Edwin Vieira, Esq., a Constitutional expert a usurper need not undergo prosecution by impeachment in order to be removed from the White House. This because a usurper is not actually in the office from which his or her removal is sought.

Obama's impeachment was never necessary because Obama is a usurper. The evidence that Obama is an imposter includes a forged Birth certificate, selective service card and the illegal use of someone else's social security number. The facts are prima facie and incontrovertible. Obama has not debunked any of the evidence against him. Obama is a fraud, usurper, traitor and spy.

The continued taciturn tolerance of the Government regarding Obama's treasonous crimes, it's failure to arrest Obama and to prosecute him is illustrative of a very corrupt system that has been allowed to fester under Obama's spurious faux "administration". If something is not done now, to indict Barack Obama, our nation is doomed to see his espionage repeated by others. It has happened twice already, If I and others didn't challenge the last elections by suing Cruz,Rubio and Jindal, it could have been the 3rd time such a usurpation of our highest office took place.

We now have a 100% American President, Donald J. Trump, Sr. Both of his parents were U.S. Citizens at the time of President's Trump's birth in New York City, N.Y. President Trump possesses both 100% American jus sanquinis as well as U.S. jus soli. Let's take proactive measures to ensure that every future President meets all of the Article II criteria, lest the tentacles of foreign nations attach themselves inextricably to our sovereign nation to our detriment and demise.

Every American citizen must be stalwart in their defense of the U.S. Constitution and our nation. We all have a sacred duty to preserve our American Republic for posterity. It was preserved for us by past generations at very great cost to lives and fortune. We were handed the torch of Liberty and must, when the time comes, pass it on for future generations to preserve. Our task is neither trivial or easy. But it is morally imperative that the United States and it's "Blessings of Liberty" survive and thrive. Each generation has the responsibility to see to it that the United States does survive and continues into the future. Freedom cannot be taken for granted.

Who's duty is it to safeguard our liberties? "We the People, the legislature, the executive and the judicial branch all have a share in that responsibility.

Like others wanting to make sure that no one would ever be able to claim lack of knowledge of the issue of Obama's ineligibility, I have written letters to many public officials.

I wrote one of those letters, as President and Founder, on official stationary of the Society for the Preservation of Democracy, to SCOTUS Chief Justice John Roberts on January 2, 2009.

Instructed by the Court Clerk on how to mail it, I placed (9) separate letter sized envelopes with a copy of the letter to Roberts in each envelope and then I individually addressed them to cach of the justices of the Court so that each Justice had a copy of the letter to Roberts. I then placed the (9) envelopes into a larger Manilla envelope and addressed it to the Clerk of the Court, U.S. Supreme Court and mailed it by certified U.S. Mail.

The subject of the letter was "Barack Obama and his status and eligibility to be the President of the United States". I informed the Justices of the controversy surrounding Obama and urged them to "enjoin Barack Obama from becoming President, if he does not establish his status as a Natural Born citizen of the U.S.A." On June 17, 2009 I took my oath of office and eligibility as an American Grand Jury "Presentment" hearing member which was empaneled to inquire into allegations made against Barack Obama. My oath was sworn to before Susan L. Caple, Notary Public, State of New York on June 17,2009.

What is a Presentment? "A presentment properly speaking, is an accusation made by a Grand Jury **of it's own mere motion of an offense upon it's own observation and knowledge** or upon evidence before it, and without **any** Bill of indictment laid before it at the suit of the Government, upon a Presentment, the proper officer of the court must frame an indictment, before the party accused can be put to answer it"- Joseph Story, famed American Jurist.

Prior to 1946 Presentments were in ubiquitous usage by the people. We have the authority to empanel these hearings on our own motion without any judicial officials or prosecutors present or involved. This is an awesome power because it gives "we the people" the power to remove corrupt public officials without interference by said corrupt official to squelch it.

Grand juries are a "body of accusers sworn to discover and present for trial persons suspected of criminal wrongdoing and as a protector of citizens against arbitrary and oppressive government action". Pursuant to the 5th Amendment a prosecution can be instituted both on a Presentment **or** an Indictment. "We the people still have this authority. It is enshrined in the 5th Amendment. In 1946 errant rule makers of the newly enacted Federal Rules of Criminal Procedure illegally, and quite unconstitutionally, deleted Presentments as one of the two ways in which prosecutions could be instituted under the fifth amendment. In an advisory committee note on the rules, note 4 stated **"Presentment is not included as an additional type of formal accusation, since presentments as a method of instituting prosecutions are obsolete, at least as concerns the federal courts".** Presentments have never been "Obsolete".

According to the late Justice Scalia delivering the Opinion of the court in U.S. v Williams, 504, U.S. 36 at 48 (1992):

"The Grand jury is mentioned in the Bill of Rights but not in the body of the Constitution. It has not been textually assigned, therefore to any of the branches described in the 1st (3) articles. It is a 'constitutional fixture in it's own right'".

"The Grand Jury is the fourth branch of the U.S. Government. We the People when sitting as Grand Jurors are as Scalia quoted…a constitutional fixture in it's own right"-Leo Donofrio, Esq.

Scalia also said that "The Grand Jury is an institution separate from the courts. Over whose functioning the courts **do not preside…**it belongs to no branch of the institutional govern-ment, serving as a kind of buffer or referee between the gov- ernment and the people…although the grand jury normally operates of course, in the courthouse and under judicial auspices, it's institutional relationship with the judicial branch has traditionally been, so to speak, at arm's length. Judges involvement in the functioning of the grand jury has generally been confined to the constitutive one of **calling the grand jurors together and administering their oaths of office. See: U.S. v Calandra, 414,U.S. 338,343 (1974).**

"We the People have the right and power under the 5th amendment of the constitution to charge this government with crimes by returning presentments regardless of whether the U.S. Attorneys or the federal judges agree with us"-Leo Donofrio, Esq.

In August of 2009 as a representative of the duly empaneled and sworn American Grand Jury, I served the presentments against Barack Obama and Nancy Pelosi on Eric Holder, then Attorney General of the United States, by certified U.S. Mail. I also served copies on NY State Senator Antoine Thomas., Chief U.S. District Court Judge R.J. Arcara., U.S. Senator Charles Schumer and others.

Others who were served were the City Court of Tonawanda, NY.,the Chief of Police,Tonawanda, NY., Ron Pilozi, Mayor of Tonawanda,NY., Byron Brown, Mayor of Buffalo,NY., and Kathleen Mehltretter, Acting U.S. Attorney for the Western District of New York. In addition, **all** (9) SCOTUS Justices and **all** 100 U.S. Senators at the time were served copies of the Presentments against Obama and Pelosi.

The charges that were investigated and inquired upon by the American Grand Jury were:

Count 1. That Obama is not eligible [to be President of the United States] under the laws of the Constitution of the United States as provided for in Article II, Sec.1.

Count 2. The Charge of treason against Obama filed by Lt. Commander Walter Fitzpatrick, III, USN (Ret.)

Count 3. A charge against the Democratic National Committee in Conjunction with Nancy Pelosi fraud, perjury and conspiracy to usurp the Presidency by fraud.

By unanimous vote **all** 273 Jurors voted to hand down Presentments against Barack Hussein Obama, Jr., Nancy Pelosi and the Democratic National Committee.

In November of 2009, after having served the Presentments on the U.S. District Court, WDNY, two months earlier in September. I swore out an AO91 against Barack Obama and Nancy Pelosi. In my complaint I said that Obama usurped the Presidency by fraud on January 20, 2009 and that Nancy Pelosi helped him do it.

I also accused Obama of giving aid and comfort to enemies of the United States, namely, his "Paternal cousin" Raila Odinga, a Kenyan Terrorist involved in the bombing of two U.S. Embassies in Kenya and Tanzania in 1998.

The complaint was notarized by Steven E. Ulmstead, Notary Public of the State of New York. Then, in February of 2010 I noticed that my Emails were being suspiciously suspended by Verizon after having sent emails to the 100 US Senators.

From early on, after serving the presentments on many public officials and I mean "everybody and his Uncle", **few gave a damn about Obama's usurpation.** No one wanted to handle that hot potato. U.S. Attorney Mehltretter most likely filed it in the "circular file". James P. Kennedy, Chief of the Criminal Division in her office acknowleged receipt of the complaint against Obama but then cited the FRCrimP as to why the office was "**not allowed to accept criminal complaints**". As explained earlier, the FRCrimP were compromised in 1946.

Courts make all kinds of excuses for not dealing with these authentic and bona-fide complaints. This time it was Kennedy finding loopholes and excuses for doing nothing, saying that sworn complaints made before a Notary, (notably,a person entrusted to take oaths for documents that are used in courts) was "not sufficient", citing U.S. ex rel. Spader v Wilentz.

Of course! The courts have been shoring up for years that protective wall that they have erected against the audacity of "We the people" exercising our constitutional rights. "We have a republic. If we can keep it" said Ben Franklin. It is incumbent on all of us to take constructive proactive measures in order that we may "keep" our American Republic.

I wanted to perfect my charges against Obama but was being stonewalled. I wrote a letter to in February 2010 to all the Judges and Magistrate Judges in the Western District of New York mostly to no avail. I wrote U.S. Magistrate Judges Kenneth Schroeder.,Leslie Foschio.,Hugh Scott.,Jeremiah McCarthy and Victor Bianchini. The Chief Judge R.J. Arcara was also sent the same letter. My sworn and notarized charges were being rejected but none of the Judges would allow me to swear out my charges before him. That is not the way that the United States judicial system is supposed to work. Magistrates Schroeder and Foschio redeemed themselves however. I was given very good advice by the two.

Assistant U.S. Attorney, Kennedy asked me to "Please... not contact" him "anymore regarding this matter". How's that for dedication on his part? I later received a letter from Magistrate Judge Foschio in March of 2010 referring me to Magistrate Judge Hugh Scott and further advising me that "generally federal offenses are to be prosecuted by the U.S. Attorney in the Judicial district where offense was committed". That district was the U.S. District Court-District of D.C. and the Office of the U.S. Attorney for that district, Ronald C. Machen, Jr., who was <u>a Barack Obama contributor.</u> Of course, he sat on it also. Nothing was done about the charges.

I was still at that time corresponding with the Judges and Magistrates at the U.S.D.C.-WDNY. I contacted Judge William Skretny in March, 2010 to apprise him of what had contemporaneously transpired. I had been told by Magistrate Judge Schroeder that I should contact Law enforcement with my complaint. The FBI said that they "don't take complaints" and the Secret Service also declined to take any complaint against Obama. A charge with ICE, against Obama was filed by me at the time.

On the advice of Magistrate Schroeder, off I went to local law enforcement people, namely the Police in the City that I lived in, the City of Tonawanda, NY. I filed that troublesome charge against Obama with the COTPD. As for most of the federal Judges and federal Law Enforcement Officials that I contacted I had never seen such efforts at passing the buck. However, the Chief of the City of Tonawanda NY **took my complaint against Obama. (City of Tonawanda, NY Police Complaint # 10-002-896., which he later sent to the DC Police** at my request.

The USDC-WDNY was apprised on April 7, 2010 that I filed my charges with the Tonawanda, NY Police and that I provided them with a "Preliminary Criminal Information" against Obama. I also filed it with US Attorney for DC, Ronald Machen on that date, as well as with ICE. Assistant US Attorney for the WDNY, James Kennedy was also sent a copy.

Historically the "Right to petition the government for redress of grievances has been considered the primary right"- U.S. v Cruiksank, 92, US, 542, 522 (1876). Today "the right to petition has expanded… no longer confined to redress of grievances but comprehends demands for an exercise by the government of it's powers in furtherance of the interest and prosperity of the petitioner and their views of politically contentious issues"-Eastern R.R. President's Conference v Noerr Motor Freight, 365 US. 127 (1961).

The Right to petition the government for redress of grievances extends to…the courts, as well as [to] **all departments of government.**- Cal. Motor Transport Co. v Trucking Unlimited 404 US. 508, 500 (1972) and NAACP v Claiborne Hardware Co. 458 US 886, 913-15 (1982).

An FBI Complaint which, according to agents in the Buffalo, NY FBI Office, aren't taken by the FBI, constitutes such a petition for redress of grievances. According to an FBI publication the FBI's

"Mission is to help protect you, your communities, and your businesses from the most dangerous threats facing our nation-from international and domestic terrorists to spies on U.S. Soil…from cyber villains to corrupt government officials…from mobsters to violent gangs… from child predators to serial killers…[FBI agents] work with law enforcement and intelligence partners across the country and around the globe".

According to that same publication Special Agent Patrick Bohrer, then the assistant section Chief of the FBI's Public Corruption/Civil rights program said that public corruption is "high on the FBI's list of investigative priorities".

The publication goes on to state that "Public corruption is a breach of trust by federal, state or local officials often with the help of private sector accomplices…corrupt public officials undermine our country's national security…safety, the public trust and confidence in the U.S. government, wasting billions of dollars along the way".

It was August of 2010 when 3,150 complainant signatories including myself (Signatory #1501) sent a formal complaint to former FBI Director Robert Mueller,III. In the complaint Muller was told that "We undersigned citizens have grave concerns about the existence of a domestic enemy currently controlling our government. The lawless subversion of our constitutionally based government was converted into a competing form of government through other then constit-utional means".

The complaint went on to cite "Extreme levels of corruption within the Obama administration…as Director, you are personally charged with maintaining governmental compliance within the rules of law as first and foremost defined by the provisions of the Constitution of the United States of America…the conduct of those involved leads us to conclude that the crimes of Treason, Bribery and other high crimes and misdemeanors…have been committed against both the constitution and the people of the United States of America".

Several very serious charges were lodged against Barack Obama and others. "These matters can no longer be considered to be politics as usual. The Obama administration has deliberately blurred the lines between politics and subversion so as to mask what seems to be the intent of this subversive agenda…to destroy our constitutional form of government…we see evidence of the progress of this strategy on a daily basis…"

Thirty one hundred and fifty U.S. Citizens "call[ed] upon Mueller "to exercise the full range of [his] authority and to launch an immediate investigation into these critical matters as they relate to the rule of law…Specific issues [were] enumerated" in the (75) page complaint which included the names of the 3,150 signatories to it.

Further citing that "we under[stood] the gravity of the conflicted position in which [Mueller found himself]., the FBI, as well as [Mueller] personally" we told Mueller that we were "counting on" him "to perform the functions [of his] job, consistent with [his] role as Director of the FBI, and not to **permit obvious political considerations to cloud or color [his] Judgement"**. Currently, in 2017, Mueller finds himself again in a situation in which he must do the same. To guard against his permitting "obvious political considerations to cloud or color [his] judgement" as a special prosecutor. Mueller cannot claim that he knows nothing about the complaint filed against Obama in 2010. We the People have 3,150 witnesses. What did Mueller do about that complaint filed in 2010, a full seven years having past since he was apprised?

There were (31) separate enumerated charges against the Obama "administration" ranging from the purchase of a ten foot lot from Tony Rezko for $104,500 to Treason. Such charges as campaign fraud, voter intimidation, violation of bankruptcy laws, voter discrimination, whistleblower retaliation, attempted bribery and bribery, misrepresentation, circumventing congressional authority, abuse of power (10 counts), violation of court orders, Constitutional abridgement and several others.

The most serious charge was the usurpation of the Presidency of the United States by fraud, during time of war which constitutes both espionage and treason. A capital offense, if convicted. Again, just what did Mueller do about these formally lodged complaints from over three thousand people?

I think he pulled a Schultz., "I see nothing. I hear nothing".

Meanwhile, The Joint Chiefs of Staff Chairman General Dunford was sent a copy of a **recent letter** written, this year (2017) to President Trump. The AG of the U.S., Jeff Sessions was also given a copy of the letter to Trump. It was a letter outlining the necessity of arresting Barack Obama for his longstanding crimes. In December of 2010 the Department of Defense was served a complaint against Obama written by me. There are several military officers who have spoken out about Obama's usurpation of the Presidency. For doing so, they have been retaliated against and imprisoned by Obama.

It is illegal to retaliate against a whistleblower for disclosing abuse, mismanagement, violations of law and circumstances that can affect public health and safety. Not to mention disclosing information believed to show that our national security is at risk.

Such diligent people as Colonel Lakin, Lt. Cmdr. Fitzpatrick and Lt. Easterling did their duty under Article 99 of the UCMJ which makes it mandatory to protect one's command from being taken by the enemy. These officers helped to raise awareness of the fact that Barack Obama, is constitutionally barred from being President of the United States, because he is not an Article II (USConst.) "Natural Born Citizen. Obama did on January 20, 2009 illegally enter into said office without legal authority or bona-fides,with grave disregard for the Constitution, with intent to overthrow the U.S. Government.

Executive Order #11222 Sec. 101 states:

> "Where government is based on the consent of the governed, every citizen is entitled to have complete confidence in the integrity of his government. Each individual officer, employee or advisor of government must help to earn and must honor that trust by his own integrity and conduct in all official actions"

Integrity in Government under Obama took a nose dive. Bogus Barry cannot be trusted. As a Muslim Obama is taught that lying in order to advance Islam is perfectly fine. Islam even has a name for that. It is called Taqiyya. Obama is a master muslim taqiyyist., a mendacious liar.

Australian News picked up the story of my efforts writing in March of 2011 that a "U.S. Veteran files police complaint-Obama accused of electoral crimes".

Obama spent over $2 million dollars hiding his background and his records. "Obama has come under substantial scrutiny since his rise to national prominence" says Gary Kreep, Esq.

of the U.S. Justice Foundation.

Several charges had been lodged against Obama by Dr. Kreep such as False personation of an officer or employee of the U.S., 18USC, 912., Conspiracy to commit offense or defraud the United States 18USC, 371., Activities affecting armed forces during war 18USC, 2388 (a)., False statement in application and use of Passport, 18USC, 1542., False personation of Citizen of the United States, 18USC 911 and Perjury, 18USC 1621.

In response to the Australian News article I said "It is with intense gratitude that Australia.TO has acted in behalf of the United States of America in aiding "We the People" of the USA to expose Barack Obama as a fraud and a criminal. The entire world is affected by the situation in America. Barack Obama has never been President of the United States". I left a link to a story I wrote on the Post and Email called "There is no 'President' Obama" which can be accessed by googling or by searching the Post and Email archives under my name.

My efforts to bring Obama to the bar of Justice continued when I wrote the Federal Elections Commission about Obama's legal encumbrances to being President. Primarily, he is barred by the Constitution. A letter I wrote on Society letterhead to Cynthia Bauerly, then Chairwoman of F.E.C. was copied to Caroline Hunter, Vice-Chair., Matthew Petersen, Commissioner., Donald McGahn,

Commissioner, Steven Walther, Commissioner and Ellen Weintraub, Commissioner.

My letter met with the same ubiquitous government tactic of passing the buck. I should contact the "Election assistance commission, State's Secretary of State or Local Election Board" said Jeff Jordan, Esq. of the F.E.C.

I've done all three of those things. I filed Ballot Access Challenges in New York State and New Hampshire. I sent a copy of a December, 2011 Ballot Access Challenge contemporaneously to Eric Holder, then AGUS and to James Walsh, Co-Chair, NY State Board of Elections in Albany,NY.

The Erie County, NY Board of Elections was notified at the same time in a "Notice" that read "I have formally filed a ballot access challenge against the inclusion of Barack Obama on the 2012 Presidential Election Ballot in NY. Reason: Election fraud, treason and failure to qualify constitutionally".

Laurie Barone,NY State Assembly Commission on Election Law was contacted and apprised of these challenges in January of 2010. I told her that Obama stood accused of treason "by bona-fides American Citizens, including myself" and that for "No reasonable legal rationale [those charges] have not been addressed by those in authority to do so", I further said that "a failure to adjudicate these charges constitutes dereliction of duty and malfeasance...it's a matter of national security". I told her of the deleterious effect such nonfeasance has on the nation and criticized Supreme Court Justice Clarence Thomas who told Congressman Serrano in open hearing that SCOTUS is "Evading the issue".

I told Barone that "Instead of being appalled the entire room burst into raucous laughter" and I then asked her "What...is funny about misprision of felony and treason?" and by the U.S. Supreme Court, no less. At the time "there [were active] ballot access challenges being lodged against Obama in **all 50 States...**I urge your committee to not allow him to usurp the presidency...**a second time**".

When such a precarious situation exists that there is an imposter in the oval office, there is such a level of danger to our national security that every American is duty bound as a citizen to speak out about it and to tell "everyone and his uncle" about it. Lives have been lost in our short history. Our nation is still vulnerable to foreign and domestic attack by both quislings and spies. I apprised such other persons as NY Assemblymen Cusick and Schimminger as well as Governor Andrew Cuomo. Noteworthy is the fact that "the Attorney General of the State of New York is the counsel for the sovereign State of New York, and since the NYS-BOE is a creation of an Amendment in the current NYS constitution [in 2012] the NY State -OAG **is also counsel** for the entirely privately managed board as if it was a State agency staffed by public State of NY workers"-Bill Van Allen "The NYS-BOE is staffed entirely by employees under total membership and selection control of private parties…the NYS Democratic Party State Committee and the NY State Republican Party State Committee" according to Van Allen.

How can that not be a conflict of interest?

Congress and the Senate were also formally notified of my very serious concerns regarding Obama and the grave threat that he presented in 2012 and which he still presents to our nation's security. Copies of a July 2012 letter to Congress was sent to Rep. Louise Slaughter., Sen. Charles Schumer., Sen. Kirsten Gilibrand., John Boehner, Speaker of the House and then rightful President of the United States and Daniel Inoye, U.S. Senate President, pro tempore.

One of the charges against Obama is that he usurped the Presidency by fraud during time of war. To that charge, I filed a formal complaint with the Department of Defense. Obama is guilty of espionage under 10USC, Sec. 906, Art. 106 in that he, without any legal authority or bona fides as President to do so, unlawfully accessed Top Secret and above military secrets and entered into areas, [while impersonating the President of the United States] wherein the conduct of war, during time of war, was being engaged in. Barack Obama was made aware of this.

I wrote a letter directly to Barack Obama on February 22, 2012. This was around the same time that a "Birther Summit" was being planned. The Summit was later cancelled. In any event I told Obama that he was "not the bona-fides President of the United States...[&] the subject of several ongoing investigations being undertaken to determine who [he really is]". I asked him to "clarify the issue of [his] ineligibility to be President by divulging all the records that [he] has attempted to keep secret".

I reminded him of the Presentments against him which were served on Eric Holder in which he is accused of several crimes including treason. I said that he was "being scrutinized...for [his] support of terrorists in Kenya, [his] support of Zakat, Sharia [Law]" and "[his] Islamic supremacism and other anti-American activities.

I continued the letter by disputing his claim to be a Christian telling him that it "is of such a mendacious nature that it totally lacks any credibility or foundation in fact". Pointing out several significant reasons why he could not be believed, I cited his having publicly mocked the Judeo-Christian Bible while calling the Islamic Q'uran "Holy", his deference to Islam and blasphemies against Jesus and God of the Bible. I told him that God of the Bible is not the same entity as allah. God of the Bible and allah are not the same entity, the same being. God of the Bible exists while allah does not.

Obama has had U.S. troops in Afghanistan burn Bibles so as not to offend Muslims while ordering them to wear white gloves when handling the Q'uran. Has anyone ever seen a Muslim in Saudi Arabia handle the Bible with white gloves? I informed Obama that I was a Federal retiree who had worked for (3) decades for the Federal Government and that I had many dealings with past presidents in my capacity as a Union official. I told him that I did not trust him and that he was a "Mysterious individual fraught with many unanswered questions about [his] dubious past history" and that he has "been exposed as a fraud and...accused of treason and espionage".

In the February, 2012 letter from me as President of the Society for the Preservation of Democracy and Human Rights, Obama was reminded of a previous formally served "Notice of Citizen's Arrest" upon Presentments and that he should consider himself under arrest. He was apprised that I knew I could not enforce my citizen's arrest and physically arrest him but that one day "someone in law enforcement" would.

I went on for another page in which I cited the Statutes for treason & being a spy respectively.,18USC, Part 1,Chapter 115, Sec. 2381 & 10USC, Sec. 906 Article 106. I copied the letter to Biden, Boehner & Inuoye, who were at the time next in succession as POTUS.

Getting back to Obama's claim that he is a Christian and not a muslim. There is more evidence that he is lying about his Christianity. The fact that he wears a ring with the words "allahu akbar" on it. He's had the ring for years. He takes it off during the Islamic "holy" season of Ramadan, when it is not permitted to wear jewelry.

Obama claimed that we were "Not a Christian Nation" saying more than once that "we are a Muslim nation". Obama speaks fluent Arabic and has stated in the past that "the Islamic call to prayer [the adhan] is the most beautiful sound on Earth". Christians do not say these things nor act in these ways nor do they call the Q'uran "Holy" or praise allah. Our current Pope, Francis must be prayed for. I believe that he is confused about any perceived or purported religious link between Christianity and Islam. Given the recent threats made against the Vatican by Muslims, he should realize that we have no links to the satanic false religion of Islam. They want "Infidels" DEAD!!.

Let me point something out. Arabic has no letters or characters that are capitalized or stand out as more significant than others. The word "allah" should not be capitalized in English. The word allah may mean "god" but it does not mean "God" with a capital "G" as in "God" of the Bible. The term allah is generic for god. A "god" is a false idol. God of the Bible exists while allah does not. It is a major mistake to conflate God of the Bible with allah of the Q'uran. They are not one and the same. Islam claims Jesus, whom they call 'isa, as being the "Penultimate Muslim prophet" while placing muhammad at a higher level than him and subsequently, muhammad below allah as allah's prophet. In the Bible Jesus is the Son of God. Christians believe that Jesus is God incarnate and have explained this by the concept of the Holy Trinity. Muslims deny 'isa (Jesus) is God and say

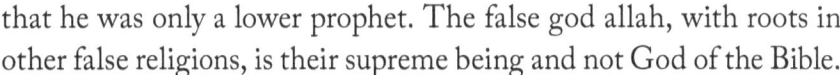

that he was only a lower prophet. The false god allah, with roots in other false religions, is their supreme being and not God of the Bible.

Muslims believe that Jesus did not die but was taken up to heaven alive. I am of the belief that mohammad cherry picked precepts of the Bible and **invented Islam.**

That Christians, Jews and Muslims worship the same God is patently false and ludicrous. Judaism, Islam and Christianity have been linked together quite erroneously as the "Three Abrahamic religions". Fact is that Islam is **not a religion at all.** A very interesting book has been written about Islam. The book is called "Slavery, Terrorism and Islam" by Dr. Peter Hammond. There are also several videos on Youtube called "What Islam is Not" and "FITNA" that the reader should view.

Obama, **is undoubtedly a Muslim.** Once in an interview with ABC's George Stephanopoulos, Obama made reference to being Muslim. Obama stated "My Muslim Faith...". Without missing a heartbeat Stephanopoulos quickly interjected "You mean your Christian faith." Obama responded "My Christian faith". That didn't save him from what he said however, Obama's Freudian slip was now on record.

The question is, why does Obama so adamantly deny his "Muslim faith". Obama does not want people to know that he is a Muslim for some reason. Is he ashamed of being Muslim, is he denying it as a Taqqya maneuver? The reason is because it was Saudi money that aided Obama's insinuation into the American political sphere. According to a 2012 article in Investors Business Daily, Obama got financial assistance from a person named Khalid-Abdullah Tariq al-Mansour aka David Warden, an anti-Israel advisor to Saudi Prince and billionare Waleed bin Talal. The Saudis were seeking to exert influence in the United States. One Vernon Jarrett, the father in law of Valerie Jarrett who has been called the "Consigliare to the Obama White House", wrote a 1979 article called "Will Arabs back ties to Blacks with cash?". OPEC had been approached by Mansour with the proposal that they be involved in disbursing $20 million dollars per year for (10) years to aid 10,000 minority students like Obama.

The beneficiaries of this arab OPEC fund money would then be expected to "migrate through the [U.S.] political system **promoting Palestinian and radical islamist causes". Obama would be acting as an agent of a foreign nation, quid pro quo.**

John Charlton of the Post and Email wrote a very telling article called "A Chronology of forgery and Deceit. How a crude forgery was passed off as authentic to get an unknown elected as President of the United States". Dated January 27, 2010.

Mr. Charlton cited in his story that the Israelis had discovered that Obama's COLB (Certificate of Live Birth) "lacked proper accompanying marks of authentication" and the required attestation of "accepted by Registrar". As early as 2008 the Israelis were claiming that Obama's birth certificate was a forgery. This fact has been to date proven as true. Obama's proffered birth certificate is indeed a forgery as determined by several independent forensic document experts as part of a cold case posse investigation conducted by former SherifJoseph Arpaio of Maricopa County,Arizona, himself the victim of government whistleblower retaliation. One very interesting point Mr. Charlton made was that Obama's COLB referred to him as "Barack Obama,II" instead of Barack Obama, Jr. yet no one else in the time between 1961 and the time the forged COLB was introduced has ever referred to Obama as "Obama,II". That started only after he proffered the forged COLB which had "Obama,II" written on it.

I have written to all my representative in the House of Representative and the Senate. My Congressman is Higgins. My Senators are Schumer and Gillibrand. They couldn't care less about what Obama did. They probably helped him. It's reminiscent of the story of the "Emperor's New Clothes".

by Hans Christian Andersen. Everyone knows or should know, that "We the People" have been fleeced. Not many want to admit it or even care. They probably have a quid pro quo arrangement also.

They would rather walk around in a vulnerable situation, with their pants down, so to speak. That thought brings to mind how it has become a widespread fashion statement for young black men to wear their pants around their thighs versus their waists. Fools.

Obama must be arrested and tried for his crimes. It is a moral imperative. At a time when stricter attention to enforce the Constitution is necessary, due to Obama's blatant and widespread abrogation of it, Congress has been trying instead to erode the Article II requirement that a President be a "Natural Born Citizen". I have great reason to thank God this Thanks Giving Day that the several efforts by Congress to do so (at least 8 times since 1975) have met with abject failure. Americans, in their great wisdom, simply do not want the "Natural Born Citizen" requirement scuttled. They know that if it were, foreign influence of the kind al-Mansour exercised under Obama would continue to occur, allowing foreigners wanting to ruin the United States or control it, to run amok.

I myself have taken my cases through the NY State Court System twice already. I am currently going after NY State for misrepresenting the criteria for being President as explained earlier in this book. In March of 2014 I was in the Supreme Court of the United States with my first case, Laity v NY, # 13-875. The Justices denied my Writ of Certiorari.

The silver lining in this was the fact that this meant that the four SCOTUS precedent cases affirming that a "Natural Born Citizen is one born in the United States to parents who are both U.S. Citizens themselves" **was left undisturbed.** A subsequent Petition for rehearing was also denied in May, 2014. May 15th, 2014 was when my City of Tonawanda NY Police case against Obama (#10-002-896) was forwarded to Chief Lanier of the DC Police by the Chief of the Tonawanda Police. I alleged a violation of DC Code 22-1404, inter alia.

Several DC law enforcement officials, as well as the Mayor of DC, were sent copies of my complaint. See: DC Police #T14002751 from June, 2014 and DC Office of Police Complaints., Complaint # 14-0294. OPC contact was Sergeant Rodney Ervin of the MPDs OPC Liaison Unit. A letter sent to me stated that my complaint had been referred to the Metropolitan Police Department for whatever action they deem appropriate". That letter was signed by Mona Andrews, Chief Investigator of the OPC. The FBI was contacted again by me in July,2014. They had done nothing that I could see to address the previously submitted formal charges against Obama, with 3150 signatories on it, including me.

Even the International Criminal Court in the Hague had Obama in it's radar. ICC conducted investigations into the Kenyan Presidential elections in which Obama actively campaigned, as a U.S. Senator, for Raila Odinga., a person who claimed that he was "Obama's paternal cousin".

Fast forward to September,2016 the time I wrote an Email to Channing Philips, U.S. Attorney for D.C. The contents of that message is as follows:

"Subject: Renewal of Criminal Complaint against and citizen's arrest of Barack Obama by the undersigned complainant circa 2012... Channing Phillips...This will confirm a telephone contact I made to your office recently wherein I requested a status report regarding the above captioned matter, the usurpation of the presidency by Barack Obama in 2008 and 2012 in violation of the DC code and other statutes regarding 'impersonation of a public official', espionage and treason.

I sent said complaint to your predecessor, Ronald C. Machen, Jr. after having contacted the DC Police, complaint # T1400-2751 on the advice of U.S. Magistrate Judge Leslie Foschio, USDC/WDNY. I will be following up with a letter to you soon.

There has been an emerging pattern. There were (3) Three Candidates in the 2016 Presidential election that are also not Article II, Sec. 1 "Natural Born Citizens". They are Ted Cruz, Marco Rubio and Bobby Jindal. The U.S. Supreme Court has defined a "Natural Born Citizen" as one born in the United States to parents who are both U.S. citizens themselves. Neither Obama, Cruz, Jindal, Rubio or McCain meet these mandatory constitutional requirements".Then I signed it and sent Copies of this missive to the DOJ, Donald McGahn, Esq.,

Michael Cohen, Esq., Greg Rogers., Sharon Rondeau., Mildred Mang and Donald J. Mang. All of my various efforts are part of the public record. A simple google of my name will serve to verify everything that I have written here. I cannot stress the following enough:

The national security of the United States of America under Obama's faux "administration" was in a situation of extremely clear and present grave danger. The time has come to pass when individuals who had no legal right to be our president have already served multiple terms, namely Barack Obama and Chester Arthur.

Worse yet. There are persons in the wings waiting to do it again. Marco Rubio, Ted Cruz, Bobby Jindal and Arnold Swarznegger have all already tried it. These continual attempts to flout the Constitution have got to be stopped.

It is a moral imperative if we want to keep our nation.

The preservation of our American Republic for posterity is of the utmost importance. The continued existence of our American Republic is at stake if we sit back and do nothing.

Where is Obama these days. I haven't seen him in the News lately and I watch a lot of news. Things are getting hot for the Clintons and their corruption reached to that imposter in the oval office. Obama is the ringleader. Obama's purported mother was born in Ft. Leavenworth, Kansas. It is very apparent that Obama belongs in the prison there and my opinion is that he should die there. Given the nature and seriousness of the crimes that he stands accused of, Obama should face a military firing squad. Obama statues should be taken down, schools with his name on it should change the name, his Nobel peace prize should be reclaimed, people who received medals from him should request reissuance by President Trump. What a national disgrace Obama is. Hillary and Bill Clinton should also be in jail. Crime in the faux Obama 'administration", a RICO Cabal, ran rampant. Only because of complicity by some and apathy by others. God save our American Republic.

"We have a Republic if we can keep it"-Benjamin Franklin

-The End-